Pol002

VISION Paperbacks

First published in Great Britain in 1998 by VISION Paperbacks,
a division of Satin Publications Limited.

VISION Paperbacks,
a division of
Satin Publications Limited
20 Queen Anne Street
London W1M 0AY
E-mail: 100525.3062@compuserve.com

Cover design and layout: Justine Hounam.
Typesetting and design: Pixel Press.
Printed and bound in Scotland by:
Caledonian International Book Manufacturing Ltd
Photography Rex Features

ISBN: 1-901250-20-2

PRAWN COCKTAIL PARTY

The Hidden Power of New Labour

Robin Ramsay

THE AUTHOR

Robin Ramsay has been the editor and publisher of the magazine Lobster since 1983. He was the co-author of Smear! Wilson and the Secret State (Fourth Estate, 1991) and contributed to The Wilson Governments 1964-70 (eds. Coopey, Fielding and Tiratsoo, Pinter Publishers, 1993).
He has written widely for the radical press.

Lobster has a Web site at:
http://www.knowledge.co.uk/xxx/lobster/

The author can be contacted at:
214 Westbourne Avenue, Hull, HU5 3JB
tel 01482 447558
or e-mail robin@lobster.karoo.co.uk

ACKNOWLEDGEMENTS

The author is grateful to John Booth, Tom Easton, Anthony Frewin and Scott Newton for their input over the years; to Larry Elliot and Dan Atkinson of the Guardian's economics team for not surrendering; to Peter Dale Scott for showing me how this ought to be done; to Peter Hounam for thinking this worth the effort; and to Sally Walker, not least for her proof-reading skills.

CONTENTS

INTRODUCTION

This book is about the rise to power in this society of the financial sector, the City, with help from their friends overseas, and its struggles en route with Labour and Conservative Governments. If this sounds complex it is and is not. At one level it is relatively simple: one section of society, chiefly concerned with moving money, has cheated the other sections. It has been one of the greatest 'scams' ever pulled. This is a kind of hidden history, not because the facts have been hidden but because the interpretation this book contains has rarely made it into the mainstream political agenda of this society.

You can see where the power lies in a society by what is *excluded* from the political agenda. In America, after the shooting of John F. Kennedy in 1963, organised crime was off the agenda for 20 years. Do I think American politicians were afraid? Yes, I do; but afraid less of being whacked by the mob, than of having too much attention paid to the various alliances between electoral politics and organised crime at local and national level.

These alliances were hinted at when the Watergate burglar, former CIA officer, and member of 'the plumbers', John McCord, was in court for his part in the fumbled break-in at the Watergate complex. His lawyer, Gerald Alch, read out the titles of various memoranda, including 'The Mafia and the Democratic National Committee Funds and Personnel' and 'Israel and the Mafia', written by McCord, which McCord proposed to deliver to the Watergate Senate Committee, chaired by Democrat Sam Ervin.

I have no idea how solid McCord's information was – it might have been a bluff: in any case, it did not work perfectly – but he evidently thought it a threat worth making.[1]

In this country for most of the post-war era – and especially since the Tories took office in 1979 – the financial sector has been off the mainstream political agenda.[2] Considering the damage it has done, this is remarkable, bizarre and surreal.

It is remarkable politically. After all, everybody hates their bank – or knows someone who hates their bank. Most people would not need too much instruction to see that the billions of profits made by banks have come from their pockets; two to three million people were fraudulently sold private pensions in the 1980s.[3] The financial sector is a sitting duck; and until the advent of 'New Labour', the Tories were the party of the financial sector. Throughout the 1980s, as we were being exploited, the thieves' allies were on public display, most days of the year. Yet the other mainstream parties rarely, if ever, mentioned this. As Mrs Thatcher would have said, they were 'frit'.

To understand where we are now, politically, we have to go back to the 1970s. For the 1970s led to Mrs Thatcher, which led to the progressive collapse of the Labour Party as a radical, reforming party.[4] Mrs Thatcher claimed legitimacy from the events of the 1970s. There is a curious symmetry here: the insurgent wings of both political parties at the end of the 1970s were dominated by myths of betrayal. The Tory Right believed Edward Heath betrayed true Toryism with his so-called U-turn, the attempt at an incomes policy, his Industry Bill, the arrival of the Ugandan Asians, the explosion of inflation and so forth.[5] The

---

[1] I believe none of these memoranda were ever published: they may never have been written. New York Times 1973 p. 190. See Bibliography for citation sources.

[2] They remained on the agenda of the far right, the NF et al, and flitted in and out of that of the Communist, Trostskyist and anarchist left.

[3] The widespread use of the term 'mis-selling' well illustrates the dominance of the agenda by the financial sector. 'Mis-selling' was promoted by the financial sector to distract us from the fact that it was a fraud, pure and simple.

[4] Labour was never a socialist party; not even in the early 1980s.

[5] In a retrospective on the Heath years, Sir Geoffrey Howe spoke of 'the sense of betrayal which was felt by people like Nicholas Ridley, and Jock Bruce-Gardyne and Ian Gow,' all important members of the Thatcher group. Journalist Hugo Young said 'the dynamism of Thatcherism related to what is adherents perceived to be the betrayal of what had happened at Selsdon Park.' Kandiah (ed) pp 191/2.

Labour Left believed the Wilson-Callaghan governments of the 1970s betrayed socialism with the IMF crisis, cuts in public spending, attacks on the unions, the introduction of monetarism and so forth.[6]

Behind the Left's betrayal myth is the perception of British economic failure. But as Ross Gibbon and Artis, Cobham and Wickham-Jones [7] have pointed out, at this distance the Wilson-Callaghan Governments of the 1970s look rather successful. All the Western industrialised economies had trouble in the 1970s coping with the rise in the price of oil; but that OPEC-initiated inflationary push was grossly amplified in the UK by the Heath-Barber boom, preceded by the first burst of financial deregulation and ensuing massive expansion of domestic credit by the British banks. Hence inflation was approaching 20% and rising when Harold Wilson took over from Heath in 1974. It is too often forgotten that the rise of the monetarists within the Tory Party in the 1970s was a response not to Labour policy, but to the Heath-Barber monetary 'incontinence' as Mrs Thatcher puts it in her memoir.[8]

In 1974 Labour inherited the mess and tried to bring down inflation without a massive recession. And on the whole they were pretty successful. Yes, living standards fell a little – an inevitable consequence of a sharp rise in the cost of a basic commodity like oil – and public spending was reduced. And yes, the IMF came in and lent the government some money. But even

---

[6] The betrayal theme on the Labour Left is discussed in 'Social Democracy in Hard Times', Mr Artis, D. Cobham and M. Wickham-Jones in 20th Century British History Vol. 3, no. 1 1992, p. 33.

[7] 'Homage to Wilson and Callaghan' in London Review of Books 24 October 1991. For Artis et al, see note 6 above. Another expression of the same point is in 'Jim Nearly Fixed It', Kenneth O. Morgan, The Guardian, 4 November 1996.
The Guardian's Economics Editor, Larry Elliot pointed out that Britain's OECD ranking was 16th in the 1950s, 13th in the 1960s, and 10th in 'the much-vilified 1970s'. The Guardian July 15 1996. It is now 19th.

[8] The Path To Power, p. 299 The same expression is used by Rhodes Boyson in his 1978 Centre Forward: A Radical Conservative Programme p. 57 Neither Boyson nor Thatcher seem remotely aware of what we might call lumpen Freudianism, so neither would notice the bizarre use of the money = shit symbolism, identified by Freud, in their association of money and incontinence.

this central plank in the left myth is not as straightforward as it seemed, and still seems, to the Labour Left.

The sense of crisis surrounding the IMF loan of 1976 was of symbolic rather than actual significance. The Labour Government had been borrowing from the IMF throughout the Wilson years without a great fanfare. The memoirs of Harold Wilson and Roy Jenkins make it clear that the relationship with the IMF was simply part of normal economic life, as was intended by its creators.[9] Half the 1976 loan was never used and the rest was paid back without incident.[10] The policies promised in the 'Letter of Intent' – the contract – from the government to the IMF were of little consequence and unexceptional. As Bryan Gould pointed out, the government promised the IMF merely to maintain a competitive pound and conduct monetary policy by reference to an IMF-favoured indicator, Domestic Credit Expansion.[11] The cuts made in public expenditure demanded by the IMF would have been made anyway;[12] and at the end of the negotiations, the IMF had got much less than it initially sought from the Labour Government. (The IMF event is discussed in detail below.)

The IMF incident was just one in a series of assaults, some economic, some political, on the Labour Government between 1974 and 1979. There was an economic problem: inflation at 25% is a very serious economic problem. The Labour Government was trying to bring down inflation; and a cut in living standards was inevitable, at least in the short term, which was a serious political problem. But arguably much of the sense of 'crisis' which pervaded the mid-1970s was the result of psy-war opera-

[9] See IMF index references in Roy Jenkins (1991) and Harold Wilson (1971).

[10] See Denis Healey pp. 431-3

[11] Gould pp. 120 and 1. Gould has his own go at myth-making. 'Popular mythology has it that the IMF exacted from the Labour Government a savage programme of spending cuts. The truth is that the IMF proposed two conditions only...' (p. 120) In fact the IMF did impose cuts in public expenditure as a pre-condition of the loan. It was the cuts, not the two insignificant promises in the Letter of Intent, which caused the anguish in the Labour cabinet.

[12] James Callaghan said recently in an interview with Peter Hennessy that with or without the IMF the Labour Government would have reduced public spending. Hennessy, Muddling Through p. 285

tions by the secret services of the US and UK, their allies in the propaganda organisations of capital and the Tory Party, by elements within the Government itself, notably the Treasury, in the media and by the US Government. By the 'Winter of Discontent' of 1978/9, inflation was on the wane, North Sea oil revenues about to come on stream and boost the domestic economy and the public revenues, and the problem with sterling wasn't that it was falling but that it was rising too far.

But politics is about beliefs as well as about reality. The underlying economic belief which sprang from the 1970s experience and underpins the Right's view of the decade was, as David Owen put it, that 'The Keynesian Revolution had run out of steam – instead of maintaining full employment, it had produced high unemployment and inflation at the same time.'[13] But unemployment in the 1970s was not high by the standards of the 80s. Nor is it clear at all that the inflation of the 1970s was the result of the Keynesian revolution. In what sense did the oil price hike and the explosion of the money-lenders – the major causes of Britain's inflation – result from the Keynesian revolution? The deregulation of the banks under Heath was an expression of their determination to get back to pre-WW2, pre-Keynesian, conditions.[14] The Thatcherite picture of the 1970s, now internalised and universalised throughout the mass media and by most of the Labour Party, of a nightmare of national decline, is bolstered by the Labour Left's portrayal of the 1974-79 governments as the great betrayal. We may remember few details of the Wilson-Callaghan years but we all remember that there was 'a crisis'.[15]

---

[13] Time to Declare p. 418. Andrew Neil, erstwhile editor of the Sunday Times, put it his way: 'My country had been brought to its knees by the brute force of union power' (p. 20)... 'the dark days of pay policy, strikes and the social contract, when the unions seemed to run the country...' (p.19) ...'moderate, centre-left social democracy had been tried and failed in the 1970s, collapsing ignominiously in the 1978-9 Winter of Discontent.' (p. 387) Neil 1996

[14] This is discussed in Ewan Green.

[15] In the Guardian, 3 May 1997, a survey of the Major years by Michael White was headed by a series of little captions for each of the Tory years. For 1979, above a picture of Margaret Thatcher, it was said she took over, 'faced with a dire legacy of Labour overspending and economic mismanagement.'

Prawn Cocktail Party

This book describes the rise to power of the City of London in the post World War 2 period; its manipulation of the Heath and Thatcher Governments; Mrs Thatcher's failed attempt to resist it; and the Labour Party's progressive collapse before its power which climaxed with the election of Tony Blair as party leader and front-man for it.

This can be book-ended by two anecdotes. Some years ago, in a pub in the Lake District, I met a Brit who had been working in Canada. In his forties, he told me of a school reunion he had attended – a group of middle-aged men who had known each other 25 years before. One was a big cheese at Barclays Bank, another a businessman. The businessman asked the Barclays banker why the banks charged him 25% on his credit card. And the banker replied, 'Because we can.'

The other anecdote was told to me by a woman who worked for a time, as a lawyer, in one of the so-called regulatory bodies in the City. One day, in the mid-1980s, her boss asked her to go down to the House of Lords and listen to debate on some piece of legislation which might affect their work. 'Make sure the Labour Party aren't paying attention,' he said.

They were not.

---

2 The interests and views of the non-European Union overseas interests are best reflected in the pages of the Sunday Telegraph and largely, though not entirely, explain why that paper is so hostile to the European Union.

3 OECD figures from Larry Elliot, Guardian Economics Editor, in the Guardian 15 July 1996.

Chapter One

Operation Robot

Though there are considerable arguments about the meaning of, and relationship between, the various terms such as the City, the financial sector and finance capital, they are all attempts at a short-hand for a group of inter-related and generally mutually supporting financial institutions, whose interests lie wholly or partly outside the domestic British economy; and which, virtually unregulated and unchallenged since the Tories took office in 1979, have now established complete hegemony over the agenda of British society.[1] This nexus of interests consists mainly of the banks and insurance companies, and other major financial institutions, some British multinational companies, and the sections of Whitehall which represent their interests abroad. It would not be too inaccurate to describe it as the City plus the Foreign Office. But this nexus of interests is now divided between those whose wealth is invested inside the European Union and those whose wealth is invested outside it.

In a sense there are now three 'British economies': the domestic economy, the overseas-European Union economy and the overseas-non European Union economy. None of the terms currently in use is a satisfactory short-hand for this complex mixture, but this complexity is too cumbersome to be conveyed except at length. In this book I will refer mostly to 'the City', meaning the financial sector and the overseas lobby – this group of interests outside the UK. From the point of view of the domestic British economy, it matters little in which part of the globe

[1] There are long, complicated, academic discussions about the difference between these terms which I choose to ignore. For an introduction to the subject see Wyn Grant (ed.), chapter 4.

'British' investment is made; it just is not invested in Britain.[2]

The domestic-overseas conflict is as simple as it looks. Wealth which originated in Britain which is invested or consumed abroad does not benefit the economy of the UK as much – if at all – as it would if invested in the UK. Imagine what Britain would look like if all the wealth which originated in the UK had been invested here and not abroad! The beginning of all political discussions, in my view, should be: do we let the wealth created in the UK go abroad? It is presumably not wholly coincidental that Britain's decline from 10th in the OECD 'league tables' of economic performance to its present 19th began in 1980 when the Conservative Government scrapped all the remaining controls on overseas investment of British-generated wealth.[3] But there is almost nobody left in mainstream British politics willing to argue this case and the issue no longer makes it onto the main agendas of this society.

The economic history of Britain since 1970 has seen a continuation of the conflict between the interests of the domestic economy and overseas economy which is one of the major themes in British economic policy in the 20th century. From the rise of Tariff Reform League before World War 1, through the attempts by its domestic manufacturing-based successors such as Patrick Hannon and the British Commonwealth Union to create an 'industrial group' of MPs in the House of Commons in the immediate post WW1 period, to the climactic struggle over the reimposition of the Gold Standard, the conflict was between the interests of the financial, overseas sector with its instruments in the Bank of England and the Treasury – and the domestic economy. In the 1930s crisis a kind of compromise was reached between domestic and overseas sectors: the overseas sector accepted some controls and was largely confined to the trading bloc of the Commonwealth, the so-called sterling area.

During WW2 normal proceedings were subsumed under the

---

[2] The interests and views of the non-European Union overseas interests are best reflected in the pages of the Sunday Telegraph and largely, though not entirely, explain why that paper is so hostile to the European Union.

[3] OECD figures from Larry Elliot, Guardian Economics Editor, in the Guardian 15 July 1996.

command economy: everything, capital movements and trade, was centrally controlled. After the war the controls remained initially as the British state's paramount interest in the maintenance of its empire led to its role as truculent and subordinate partner in the Anglo-American alliance.[4] Bits of the overseas sector in London – commodity trading and shipping, in particular – picked up as post-war reconstruction produced a growth in world trade. But stock market transactions declined between 1946 and 1950 and merchant banking was static.

Key episodes in our post-war economic history show different aspects of the same struggle between the domestic economy and overseas interests. In 1948 Prime Minister Attlee and Foreign Secretary Bevin had a fight with the Chiefs of the Imperial Staff when Attlee in particular was reluctant to continue vast military spending, particularly in the Middle East and the Mediterranean, to maintain Britain's pre-war influence. In early 1948 Attlee had the temerity to tell the Chiefs of Staff that 'there was no one to fight'; but eventually he capitulated after Foreign Secretary Ernest Bevin changed his mind and accepted the line coming out of the Foreign Office,[5] and the Chiefs of the Imperial General Staff threatened to resign.[6] The same issue can be seen in the split in the Labour cabinet over the increased arms expenditure – overseas expenditure paid for by domestic cuts – proposed by Labour Chancellor Gaitskell which led to the resignation of Aneuran Bevan and Harold Wilson from the government in 1951. The de facto 'producers alliance', formed of necessity during the war, continued after the fall of the Attlee Government in 1951, but the controls on capital were only slowly loosened. The Conservative Governments proceeded cautiously in moving back to the pre-war arrangements because they were either unwilling to take the

[4] Dean Acheson was quite wrong when he famously said of Britain after Suez that it had lost and empire but not found a role. It had a role as the new school bully's best friend, trying to use American power in the various Anglo-American alliances formed during and after the war, to maintain its status in the world.

[5] Smith and Zemetica p. 251. A shorter version of the same thesis is their 'Clem – the cold war dissenter' in New Statesman 26 April 1985. Bevin was 'the great foreign secretary', acclaimed by all, precisely because he followed the Foreign Office line.

[6] Julian Lewis p. 292

electoral risk of being seen to challenge the welfare state and the post-war settlement; or because, like Harold Macmillan who succeeded Eden as Prime Minister, they believed in it.

OPERATION ROBOT

The overseas and financial lobby made one serious attempt to break free of these controls. In 1952 a little group comprising Treasury and Bank of England officials, with the support of R.A. Butler who was then the Chancellor of the Exchequer, tried to persuade the Conservative Government to make 'a dash for freedom', and move to full convertibility of sterling and float the pound. Operation Robot, as this manoeuvre was called, was resisted – Harold Macmillan, for example, called the proposals 'a bankers' ramp' – and eventually defeated. As we shall see, both in its aims and in the methods used to try and implement it, Robot was the prototype for other, later attempts to free the overseas lobby from the constraints of civil society.

Robot was put together by Sir Leslie Rowan, Second Secretary at the Treasury, Sir George Bolton, an Executive Director at the Bank of England, and Otto Clarke an Under-Secretary at the Treasury – with the support of Chancellor of the Exchequer 'Rab' Butler. Normal consultation procedures within the Bank and Treasury were ignored in what the Americans would call a bureaucratic end run. In the infantile jargon of the British civil service it was an attempt to 'bounce' the proposals through a small group of ministers, having already primed Prime Minister Churchill.[7] The papers were to be handed out on the spot, with no time for departmental consultation, for Ministers to have a quick look at – and nod through.

One of those who learned of, and opposed Robot at the time, economist Donald Macdougall commented:

'It seems there was no real intention to have a discussion of the Chancellor's proposal. It was largely a matter of informing Ministers in advance in the same way as they are informed of budget proposals shortly before a budget speech.'[8]

Unfortunately for Robot's backers, one of those present at the

---

[7] Macdougall pp. 87-9. Churchill had also been favourably briefed about the plan by the Bank of England.

[8] Ibid. p. 89

meeting of ministers had been alerted to the proposals. After an intense struggle, described in detail by Macdougall, the Robot proposals were rejected. Undeterred, the same group tried to 'bounce' a slightly amended set of proposals through the Cabinet some months later and were again resisted.[9]

The Robot proposals were breathtaking. Its authors proposed sterling leaving the post-war international system of fixed exchange rates. In so doing this would have alienated not only the United States, but also the countries of Western Europe who were involved with the UK in a payments system, and the Commonwealth who would have found most of their 'sterling balances' – money owed to them held in London – blocked. According to Macdougall the Robot plan also included 'trading arrangements that would have amounted to the most extreme form of Schactian bilateralism, similar to that practised by Germany during the Hitler regime before the war.'[10] Domestically, the Robot authors acknowledged that if implemented their proposals would lead to instability, higher interest rates and increased unemployment; and 'Rab' Butler even acknowledged that they might prevent the Conservative Party getting re-elected for 20 years! That these consequences were considered acceptable, was a measure of how much the overseas lobby and the City wanted convertibility of sterling and the abolition of exchange controls.

In his study of the Treasury, Henry Roseveare commented on 'Robot' that:

'...parallels with 1925 are not too far-fetched. Here, it seems, was the same ruthless impatience on the part of the financial authorities to submit the British economy to the automatic disciplines of international monetary pressures. Here also was the powerful alliance of the Bank of England and the Treasury's

---

[9] Ibid. p. 102 and 3. Macdougall notes that the second time 'the whole thing was presented almost as a minor technical change. It was a good exercise in false perspective but seriously misjudged the gullibility of its readers.'

[10] Ibid. p. 91 This is very curious, for as Scott Newton shows in his study of the pre-war era, The Profits of Peace, those 'Schactian' arrangements had also been favoured by a sizeable chunk of British international industry; and this section of British industry, and 'Rab' Butler, were involved in the secret attempts to reach agreement with Hitler after war had been declared in 1939.

Finance divisions... the alarming institutional breakdown that could permit a project like this get so far without the influence of the Economic Section [of the Treasury] being properly brought to bear upon it.'[11]

The same assessment as to the sources of Robot within the Treasury was made by another participant, Arthur Salter.

'When I learned early in 1952 of the new policy I was at once convinced that it had been invented and worked out with a definite plan by those who, in the Bank and the Treasury, were primarily concerned with financial and sterling policy, without the participation of those (including a section of the Treasury with such men in it as Robert Hall) who were constantly and closely connected with the direct economic consequences of any new sterling policy.'[12]

A memo written at the time by Otto Clarke, one of those promoting the scheme, stated:

'it must be in our interest to have sterling convertible for we cannot possibly trade and ship and insure and all the other things we do unless sterling is convertible'.[13]

Scott Newton commented:

'The vitality of finance and of commercial capitalism was identified with the health of the national economy. In 1951-2 and after, Britain's ruling elite considered itself to be acting in the public interest when it argued for the restoration of the liberal system it had been trained to administer. Spending cuts, de-control and convertibility did not merely represent policy options: they were the domestic and international economic expression of British liberal society.'[14]

The striking thing about 'Robot' at this distance is the similarity between its general aim of setting the bankers free, and the methods of those trying to implement it; and the successful 'bouncing' by the Bank of England of the Competition and Credit Controls through the Heath government in 1971, which is

---

[11] Roseveare p. 327

[12] Salter p. 219

[13] Cited in Newton, 1986, p.14

[14] Ibid. '...the Treasury's definition of what actually constitutes a healthy economy, has, over the long, run, constantly foregrounded the role of Britain's financial sector.' Ewan Green p. 212.

discussed in the next chapter. After the failure to whisk 'Robot' past the Cabinet, attempts to restore the City to its pre-war primacy were undertaken piecemeal and with caution, especially after Harold Macmillan became Prime Minister.[15] As speculation against the pound began to accompany the slow return of the City to its pre-war days, Conservative Chancellors responded in the pre-war manner of orthodox economics: they deflated the economy and raised interest rates, thus giving a higher return to the holders of sterling (and improving the balance of payments figures by reducing domestic consumption). The old order was returning. The cycle of speculation against the pound followed by higher interest rates, which became known as 'stop-go', reached its first climax in 1957 when interest rates were pushed up to the then extraordinary (for peace time) level of 7%.

'With the wartime and postwar control system dismantled, the only way the government could prevent a large movement out of sterling was by making Britain a thoroughly attractive place for the owners of capital.'[16] Samuel Brittan commented:

'By deflating the economy in the face of his own figures he [Chancellor Thorneycroft] was proclaiming... that production and employment would be held back whenever currency speculators decided to gamble against the pound.'[17]

The Chancellor of the Exchequer, Peter Thorneycroft, with two of his Treasury juniors, Enoch Powell and Nigel Birch, eventually resigned in January 1958 because the Cabinet would not support their demand for larger cuts in public spending. Former Treasury economist Donald Macdougall noted that Thorneycroft 'felt his only consistent supporter near the top of the hierarchy was Sir Leslie Rowan, who was in charge of external finance.'[18] Rowan was one of the three men who had tried to run Robot past the Cabinet.[19] And, in another curious illustration of the continuity of ideas and personnel, Mrs Thatcher appointed the elderly Thorneycroft as chairman of the Tory Party in 1979 while they were still in opposition – a striking affirmation of her view that

---

[15] This period is described in Newton and Porter pp. 126-30.

[16] Ibid p. 130

[17] Ibid. p. 132

[18] Brittan, Steering... p. 130

[19] MacDougall p. 96

Thorneycroft had been right in 1957.

THE OVERSEAS LOBBY

Starved of the investment which continued to go abroad, and repeatedly attacked by high interest rates and deflation – 'stop-go' – the British domestic economy was perceived to be not performing as well as its competitors – the comparisons were usually made with members of the EEC and the USA – and a long series of diagnoses of British economic failure were published in the late fifties and sixties, contributing to the climate which helped elect the Wilson government in 1964.[20] If it was true that many in Britain had never had it so good, as Macmillan famously said, it was also widely believed that we were not having it as good as the Germans or the Americans. Or the Dutch, the French or the Italians. Or even the Belgians.[21] A feature of this debate was that, unlike today, there was occasional discussion of whether or not British capital should be allowed to go abroad: capital exports were seen to be linked with Britain's relative decline.[22] But by 1971 Susan Strange was remarking on the inability of the the political system to deal with this issue.

'What is, in a way, remarkable, is that so important an aspect of economic policy should have been given so little serious attention... Indeed, none of the three main political parties in Britain has ever engaged in recent years in a serious debate on the ends or means of policy towards overseas investment.'[23]

This situation she attributed to 'a hidden bias in the political, economic and indeed social system, towards overseas investment'[24] – echoing the diagnosis of Roger Opie a few years earlier that Britain's economic problems were the result of a powerful 'overseas lobby' in Whitehall.[25] In the 1950s and 60s Britain still

---

[20] For example the Penguin Specials, British Economic Policy since the War by Andrew Schonfield (1958), Michael Shanks' The Stagnant Society (1961), and Rex Malik's 'What's Wrong with British Industry?' (1964).

[21] Malik's book (see footnote 20) p. 33 shows a table in which Britain comes tenth in Europe and America in terms of the rate of compound growth.

[22] For example in Schonfield (note 20).

[23] Strange p. 147

[24] Ibid. p. 150

[25] Roger Opie, 'The Making of Economic Policy' in Thomas (ed.)

clung to the pretensions of world power status, with all that entailed by way of overseas expenditure on diplomatic, military and intelligence activities. The 'bias' Strange detected was not so much hidden as taken for granted.

In the late fifties and early sixties the Conservatives began to think about ways of getting more growth out of the economy without impeding the City and the overseas lobby. Economic planning began to be considered. The idea of economic planning was largely imported from France which was perceived to have out-performed the UK, but the framework had barely been put in place before the 'dash for growth' attempted by Conservative Chancellor Reginald Maudling in 1962/3 resulted in the usual problem of too many imports being sucked into the economy, producing the large balance of payments deficit inherited by the Wilson Government in 1964.

The Wilson story is well known and only needs sketching here. The ambitious plans to side-step the Treasury's dominance of economic policy by the creation of Department of Economic Affairs (DEA) and the Ministry of Technology (MinTech) were frustrated because Wilson took the political decision that Labour could not afford to be in charge of the second devaluation since the war; and either simply did not perceive that to get his 'producers alliance' off the ground he would have to remove central control of the economy from the Treasury's hand, or did perceive this but felt it politically unobtainable. As Samuel Brittan noted, Wilson's eventual arrangements with the DEA and Treasury, which left the Treasury in charge of finance, 'rested on a combination of conservative illusions about the supposed autonomy of finance, and equally old-fashioned socialist ideas about the physical control of industry.'[26]

The US lent the Labour Government the funds to resist for a while the pressure for devaluation and the kind of deflationary action – essentially cuts in expenditure on public goods and services – demanded by the financial sector.[27] The 1964-67 period is a series of crises as Wilson, backed by the Americans, dodged and weaved – did not a little blackmail – and tried to borrow and fiddle his way out of the balance of payments deficit, thus main-

[26] Brittan, Steering... p. 312

[27] This is discussed in Dorril and Ramsay ch. 11

taining the value of sterling, without reducing domestic consumption enough to provoke unmanageable hostility from his party, the unions and the electorate.

After Wilson faced down the Governor of the Bank of England in 1966, with the traditional bankers' request to put up interest rates and cut spending at home, the overseas lobby began machinating, with *Daily Mirror* publisher Cecil King, then on the 'Court' of the Bank of England, as the focal point. Though the origins of King's animosity against Wilson are obscure, King, like his banker friends, wanted Wilson to cut back on domestic expenditure to 'defend the value of the pound' – the traditional rationale for sacrificing the domestic economy in the interests of the overseas lobby. One of King's allies in this was Sir George Bolton of the Bank of England who, as director at the Bank of England in charge of overseas finance, had been one of the architects of Operation Robot, discussed above.

Wilson eventually devalued in 1967 and from then on the Labour Government pursued policies of absolute financial orthodoxy in the face of recurring balance of payments deficits. Tight credit, high interest rates and cuts in public spending were the order of the day. It was in this period as Chancellor of the Exchequer that Roy Jenkins acquired the reputation for being 'sound' which made him the darling of the British establishment. In a sense, the Wilson-Jenkins austerity years paid off: by 1970 the balance of payments was in surplus; but they paid the traditional price of domestic cut-backs, rising unemployment and the wholesale disillusionment of their political supporters.

'By 1970 all challenges to the power of the Treasury had failed. In consequence Treasury rules had prevailed throughout and the government's determination to make the economy observe them had undermined the coalition which had brought it to office.'[28]

---

[28] Newton and Porter p. 159

Chapter Two

Staging a Comeback

'The Empire may have disintegrated and the UK may now be a third rate power, but the City of London has staged a comeback which would be the envy of any child movie star reaching maturity.' Professor Ira Scott, 1969 [1]

After Operation Robot in 1952, the financial sector had contented itself with the piecemeal removal of restrictions on its activities until the arrival of Edward Heath. Heath is conventionally viewed as someone who began as 'Selsdon Man', a prototype of the later Thatcher-led Tory Party. This is a false view. It is clear now that Heath had one overriding aim, entry into the EEC, and everything else played second fiddle to that.[2] In the first year and a half of his government he appeared to believe that the best way to prepare the British economy for entry into the expanded EEC was a dose of competition and freedom – the traditional Tory Party ideas of getting the government off the backs of the producers, reducing taxation and so forth; hence the Selsdon Man emphasis.

Heath believed that with these conditions, rather than by the vague notions of planning the economy held by both the Wilson Government and Wilson's immediate Conservative predecessors, British capitalism would produce the investment and modernisation required to meet the presumed bracing winds of competition from Europe. But Heath discovered that British capitalism was

[1] Cited in Reid p. 23

[2] 'The centrality of Europe to the administration's agenda was reflected in the establishment of a European Secretariat in the Cabinet Office.' Ball and Seldon p. 63.

not as enthusiastic about this as he:

'So British business had failed to respond to the new climate of enterprise which the government had striven to create after 1970. As a result, Heath now believed the government had no choice but to take an active hand itself. Two years as Prime Minister had quickly disillusioned him as to the energy and even the patriotism of British industrialists, who he felt had let him down.'[3]

This persuaded Heath 'that the government had no choice but to intervene directly to promote rapid growth – whatever ministers might have said previously about government getting off industry's back.'[4] The economist and Treasury official at the time, Donald Macdougall, witnessed the change of tack taking place:

'Then there was a sudden change in November 1972. Tony Barber, Douglas Allen and I had been invited one weekend to what we expected to be a routine meeting at Chequers with the Prime Minister. Shortly before, we were told that both the meeting and the scope of the discussion were to be enlarged: and that William Armstrong, who had been moved from the Treasury about three years before to be Permanent Secretary of the Civil Service Department, and (Lord) Victor Rothschild, Head of the 'Think Tank' (Central Policy Review Staff) set up by Heath were also going.

When we arrived, Ted started by asking William – who was obviously delighted to be back in the economic policy game again – what he thought. He said that, coming down in the car, he had been brooding over the situation and thought we should think big, and try to build up our industry onto the Japanese scale. This would mean more public spending. We should ask companies what they needed in the way of financial and other help, and give it to them.

To my surprise Ted warmed to this and said, 'Fine, and of course we must give to only to the good firms, not the bad ones...This was the occasion when Heath was converted – or at least first announced his conversion in my hearing – from a 'hands off industry' policy to one of selective intervention; and also to a major reflationary policy... William Armstrong was asked, in

---

[3] Campbell p. 452

[4] Ibid. p. 442

effect, to go away and organise some increased spending, particularly to encourage investment.'[5]

The 'brooding in the car' story was an invention. Armstrong had been heading a secret Whitehall committee since late 1971 which had been set up to devise a framework for industrial expansion. It contained members of the Think Tank, the Cabinet Office, Sir Leo Pliatzky of the Treasury and Sir William Neild, previously the Permanent Secretary at the Department of Economic Affairs of the outgoing Wilson Government.[6] Pliatzky later said of this committee: 'The concept was that we must strengthen our industrial capacity to as to take advantage of membership of the Common Market.'[7] It was this group which produced the 1972 Industry Bill which gave the state such power over industry that Tony Benn welcomed it as doing 'the spadework of socialism'.[8] This secret committee 'was an exercise of prime ministerial power comparable to Neville Chamberlain's conduct of foreign policy in 1937-9 or Eden's handling of the Suez crisis'.[9] So secret was this committee's work that even the Chief Secretary to the Treasury, Patrick Jenkin, was unaware of the Industry Bill until it was announced in the House of Commons.[10] It was this committee which produced the prices and incomes policy which followed the Industry Bill and which was to dog the Heath administration for the rest of its term in office.[11]

Heath's view of the benefits of joining the EEC extended to

---

[5] Macdougall p. 188

[6] Campbell p. 44

[7] Whitehead p. 82 'The free-marketeers among the ministers at the Department of Trade and Industry knew nothing about it [the committee] despite the detailed Industry Bill which was to emerge.' Hennessy, Whitehall p. 239.

[8] Department of Trade and Industry (DTI) Minister, Christopher Chataway, confirmed recently that EEC membership was the rationale put forward by civil servants in the DTI for the Industry Bill. See Chataway's comments in Kandiah (ed.) p. 198.

[9] Campbell p. 447

[10] Ball and Seldon p. 40

[11] 'The origins of the incomes policy of autumn 1972, according to one insider who was closely involved, can be traced to "the early summer of 1972 when William Armstrong asked Ted Heath if we could start preparing contingency plans for a new counter-inflation strategy in case inflation topped 10 per cent."' Hennessy, Whitehall p. 231

seeking to copy the institutions of EEC member states, particularly Germany.

'Heath had been very impressed, when visiting Germany, by Willy Brandt's regular round-table consultations with the unions and the German system of co-partnership; his mind began moving towards establishing a similar relationship in Britain by which the unions should be given an acknowledged role in the running of the economy.'[12]

Heath also wanted the British bankers to become more like the Germans, taking direct stakes in British manufacturing. In his diary Cecil King reports in April 1973 on having lunch with one of his friends, Sir George Bolton, then on the 'Court' of the Bank of England. Bolton told him:

'Recently Ted addressed a party of bankers at No. 10. Tuke, Chairman-designate of Barclays Bank, told him Ted had lambasted them for not investing more in British industry. This went down very badly.'[13]

Heath's only substantial biographer to date tells us:

'During 1972 and 1973 Heath became increasingly critical of what he saw as the unpatriotic caution of businessmen in the face of the opportunities which he believed the Government was creating for them... [h]e used to lecture the banks on their national responsibility, urging them to *invest directly in industry like German banks*...'[14] (Emphasis added.)

The Treasury found itself ignored by a Tory leader bent on generating economic growth. By 1972:

'Heath had no time for the Treasury's caution. He had always thought it lukewarm on Europe, and was now convinced that it systematically underestimated the benefits to be expected from joining the EEC. The 1972 Budget was framed in opposition to the Treasury, as a deliberately European policy to take Britain into the Community at full stretch.'[15]

Lord Croham, then Permanent Secretary at the Treasury, commented recently in a symposium on the Heath years:

---

[12] Campbell p. 444. He had also been impressed by Brandt's press operation and wanted to copy that too. See Ball and Seldon p. 56.

[13] King Diary 1970-74 p. 278

[14] Campbell, p. 526.

[15] Ibid p. 444. See also 'The Heath Years Symposium', Kandiah (ed.)

'There is some accuracy to the suggestion that Heath mistrusted the Treasury. In the 1960s the Treasury was less enthusiastic about membership of the European Community than Heath. This lack of enthusiasm was carried through into the 1970s. The Treasury was also quite pessimistic about the country's balance of payments outlook and the negative balance of payments effects which would be producing (sic) upon joining the Common Market.'[16]

For Heath and the little group around him EEC entry was all: the strategy was not just as a 'dash for growth', but an attempt to rejig British capitalism in preparation for EEC entry. This was not widely understood at the time, even in the Conservative Party. Norman Tebbitt, for example, writing in the mid 1980s, looked back on the Heath U-turn from the free market emphasis of 'Selsdon Man' and saw:

'a retreat into corporatism, and from there into a mish-mash of ill-considered centralist and socialist hand-to-mouth devices with no intellectual nor political cohesion marked only by fits of obstinacy alternating with climb-down.'[17]

Unfortunately British capital was not impressed by the plans of Heath and William Armstrong and chose not to follow their suggestions. One section of it in particular, the City of London, which Heath seems to have largely ignored, had other ideas.

WHEELBARROW DAYS[18]

While Heath was dreaming of kick-starting the transformation of Britain into a modern European manufacturing economy to meet the rigours of EEC membership, the City had been quietly expanding in another direction. The big expansion of City power began in the late 1960s with the development of London as an off-shore

---

[16] Kandiah (ed.) p. 196. See also Reid p. 72. 'Cabinet Office "keepers" were sent to accompany Treasury officials on some missions in case they handled things in discussions in Europe in ways that were not in line with Heath's approach.' Ball and Seldon p. 84

[17] Tebbitt p. 134

[18] 'Just take your wheelbarrow to the banks and cart away the cash' – Edward Du Cann on the credit explosion after the introduction of the Competition and Credit Control proposals of the Bank of England were introduced in 1971. Du Cann was then chair of Keysers, the merchant bank. Du Cann p. 131.

base for American money fleeing restrictions and low interest rates imposed by successive Democratic governments. Cecil King, in constant communication with the overseas sector, both as Britain's then major newspaper publisher and as a member of 'the Court' of the Bank of England, first mentions this phenomenon in his published diaries in July 1971. With banker and fellow member of the Bank of England Court, Gordon Richardson, he discussed 'the success of London as a financial centre in recent years. [Richardson] said it was remarkable and had drawn to London very numerous branches of foreign banks:'[19]

Charles Gordon, part of the management of one of the so-called 'fringe banks' in London during this period, commented later:

'The colonial expansion of overseas banks into London in the 1960s and 70s created a near ring-fenced, on-shore, unregulated lending activity, which was simply mind-boggling in its enormous size. It arose not only because of the City's laissez-faire tradition and ingrained expertise, not only because of the liberal tax aspects, not only because one or two brilliant merchant bankers, notably Siegmund Warburg, saw the fabulous possibilities early on...but because the US authorities designed their internal bank regulations almost as if they wanted to create a financial centre outside their own shores.'[20]

In the midst of this growth in the late 1960s the British clearing banks were increasingly unhappy:

'...unpaid agents of the state, bearing a great part of the considerable administrative burden of implementing exchange controls, in the post-war years their lending activities were almost constantly restricted by government, and they were the main agents through which the authorities tried to enforce periodic credit squeezes.'[21]

Chafing at their restrictions, the big clearing banks had to watch the growth of pension funds, unit trusts and building soci-

[19] He also added, 'The Jewish element in this is surprisingly very low.' King, Dairy 2 July 1974.

[20] Charles Gordon p. 152. Gordon was then running Cedar Trust, which became one of the first casualties of the secondary banking crisis of 1973/4. The role of Warburg is ironic, for Warburg was one of Wilson's few friends in the City.

[21] Moran (1981) p. 396

eties as rivals for domestic saving; the arrival of increasing numbers of foreign banks; and the rise of the so-called secondary banks which began to grow in the spaces left by the centrally restricted clearers. The Bank of England was also under pressure, for much of this financial activity was beyond their regulation; and, with the Treasury, the Bank of England set up a joint committee, under Lord Allen, to come up with a solution to these difficulties.[22]

But 'the Bank bounced the Treasury; produced its own scheme in the autumn of 1970 while the Allen committee was still pondering various options in a leisurely way.'[23] The Treasury was not happy about the Bank's proposals, believing – correctly, as it turned out – that they would produce inflation.[24] Chancellor Barber had the proposals put to him at a dinner by Governor O'Brien in January 1971;[25] and having 'bounced' the Treasury, the Bank of England 'bounced' the in-coming Conservative Government. As Margaret Reid dryly commented:

'The Bank [of England] had not overlooked the fact that the proposals accorded with the competitive ideology of the new Conservative Government.'[26]

In what were called the Competition and Credit Control proposals (C&CC hereafter) the Bank proposed that lending ceilings and liquidity minimums imposed on the clearing banks be replaced by a system of reserve assets and special deposits. There were to be no more physical or administrative controls on credit growth: market forces – i.e. interest rates; i.e. interest rate rises – would control the growth of credit. In other words, there would be an end to limits on lending, and high interest rates alone would be used to 'control' credit in the economy. Here is the authentic voice of the British banker struggling to throw off the restrictions of government and begin seriously milking the British economy. The C&CC proposals were adopted as government

---

[22] A very clear exposition of this is in Reid chapter 3. Another view is Bruce-Gardyne pp. 43 and 44. This committee is not mentioned in Chancellor Roy Jenkins' memoir of the period.

[23] Moran p. 52

[24] Reid pp. 32/3

[25] Ibid. p. 31

[26] Ibid.

policy in September 1971, barely noticed by the media or the Labour Opposition – and, if his biographers are anything to go by, barely noticed by Heath himself.[27] Indeed, at the time hardly anyone outside the higher echelons of the City seems to have known what was going on. Edward Du Cann was at a meeting of the 1922 Committee of the Conservative Party at which the C&CC proposals were described:

'I looked round the room and wondered how many of the MPs present fully comprehended what he was talking about. I doubt whether more than half a dozen had the least idea.'[28]

The proposals had been whisked through the House of Commons in Chancellor Barber's budget speech. As The Economist commented at the time, they 'had not been the subject of a single clause of legislation. Parliament has barely discussed it. It has all been fixed up as a gentleman's agreement in private conclaves in the City.'[29]

Even in the City, Du Cann tells us that:

'it was generally supposed that all that was occurring was the replacement of one system of control by another: it was certainly not appreciated, perhaps not even by the banking sector generally, that the competition part of the package meant virtually unbridled liberalism, leading to new and unforeseen risk.'[30]

A great many versions of the aim of these changes have appeared.[31] Cecil King reported a version from 'the senior official concerned with its preparation', John Fforde: [32]

'The revolution is in two parts: (1) the Bank will not support the gilt-edged market; and (2) they're now encouraging a greater degree of competition between the clearing banks...[this] should

---

[27] John Campbell, Heath's only substantial biographer to date, gives C&CC a brief mention on p. 455. The Bank of England's anodyne account of the changes was in a consultative document issued on 14 May 1971 and reproduced in the Bank of England Quarterly Bulletin, June 1971 pp. 181-193. The best discussion of C&CC is in Moran's 'The Politics of Banking.'

[28] Du Cann p. 130

[29] The Economist 'The banking revolution', 18 September 1971

30 Du Cann p. 131

[31] Michael Moran commented of C&CC that 'policies bearing the same name can signify very different things to different people'. Moran (1986) p. 44

[32] Reid p. 31

mean higher interest rates for deposits and lower rates for loans.'[33]

A contemporaneous 'spin' on C&CC, returning to Heath's desire to see more direct involvement by the British banks in industry, appeared in The Economist of 18 September 1971, 'The Banking Revolution', which presented the consequences of C&CC as being a move towards:

'the German-Japanese system of largely bank-controlled industry... a situation in which banking would have even greater control over British industry and the economy as a whole – that is, direct control through ownership and participation, rather than the indirect control it has exerted traditionally via government and the state.'[34]

Another (unstated) aim, acknowledged a decade later by the Bank of England, was to 'contract' the banking fringe, the so-called 'secondary banks', which had grown up in the sixties in the space left by the limits on the clearers' lending.[35] In the most detailed version, after noting the Bank of England's admission of the intention of reducing the banking fringe, Moran tells us that C&CC was perceived as 'a welcome if limited assertion of free market principles...' but was perceived by its principle constituency, the clearing banks as 'the end to [lending] ceilings.'[36] As banker Du Cann put it, 'the brakes were well and truly off.'[37]

It was simply the old order being re-imposed on the British economy. This was the climax of all those attempts since the post-war era to get rid of government controls. Under the new system the banks could lend what they liked and, when it was decided that there was too much credit in the system, they would put the

---

[33] King Diary 18 June 1971. Nothing illustrates King's economic naiveté better than reporting, without comment, a higher interest for savers accompanied by a lower interest for borrowers!

[34] Calling this a 'spin' is really misleading. This was disinformation, pure and simple. Nothing in the C&CC proposals could produce this interpretation. It is also interesting to see it stated that banking had 'indirect control it has exerted traditionally via government and the state'. This you do not find in the textbooks on British politics.

[35] Moran (1986) p. 50

[36] Ibid. p. 44

[37] Du Cann p. 131

interest rates up. What a truly wonderful racket! It was a coup by the Bank of England – on behalf of the clearing banks in particular and the City in general.

Having persuaded the Tories to reintroduce 'freedom' into the banking business, the clearing banks began churning their files, generating credit – literally 'printing money' – and not lending it to, or investing it in, British manufacturing as Heath seems to have expected, but to domestic consumers, to the property markets and the so-called 'fringe banks' (which in turn lent it on again, largely into property speculation).[38]

Charles Gordon, then with the secondary bank, Cedar Holdings, described the period:

'These immediate years after C&CC were wonderful shovelling times. The main thrust of the banks (there were a number of honourable exceptions) was to apply the shovel with gusto not with discretion, lip-service was mouthed to the authorities, consequences were ignored, and pious condemnations were made of those who were found out patently over-doing it. Old-fashioned lending practices were contaminated, most of the lending industry was embroiled – from the newly liberated primary banks to the reeking sewage level of the tertiary lenders.'[39]

In the absence of a memoir from Heath, it is difficult to be very clear on what he thought C&CC would do; but it seems to have been linked in his mind with the approaching entry into the EEC. As EEC entry was going to put up food prices and have other deleterious effects on the economy, Heath seems to have wanted to generate a head of steam in the domestic economy which would compensate for those effects.[40]

Heath seems to have thought that he was 'modernising' Britain, creating the conditions necessary for the transformation of Britain into a modern social democratic European country. According to the creator of Trafalgar House Investments, Nigel Broackes, who dined with Heath in January 1972, Heath said he

[38] Having complained about the activities of 'the fringe', after C&CC the clearing banks threw money at them, playing a central role in the ensuing collapse.

[39] Gordon p. 149. This chapter on the post C&CC fiasco is aptly titled 'Borrow Short, Lend Long and Go Bust'.

[40] 'The Prime Minister also wanted to see Britain's industry in better competitive shape before the country joined the EEC on 1 January 1973.' Reid p. 70.

'wanted an investment boom with an abundance of cheap credit'.[41] He certainly presided over the making of a boom, cutting personal taxes, making interest on bank loans offsettable against tax, and tripling the public sector borrowing requirement between 1971/2 and 1972/3. When the balance of payments began to suffer as a result of imports being sucked in by the boom, he floated the pound rather than slow things down (another echo of the Robot proposals). As late as September 1973, after the OPEC oil price rise, when almost everything was going wrong, Heath told a meeting of the National Economic Development Council, 'This time I am determined to swim through the whirlpool'.[42]

Heath's gamble on a dash for growth to kick-start Britain out of its stagnation did not work for several reasons. In the first place, with little commercial and no industrial experience, Heath simply did not understand British capitalism. Given the right expansionist conditions, Heath believed, British capitalism would increase investment in the domestic manufacturing economy. But it did not; and Heath took to berating those he thought should be investing – bankers, as we have seen already; and the men running the big British companies. Head of the CBI, Sir Campbell Adamson said:

'I couldn't count on the fingers of both hands the number of times that Mr Heath told us that everything had been put right that the government could put right, and still industry didn't invest enough.'[43]

How little Heath understood is suggested by his enthusiasm for Slater Walker.[44] Like many others, Heath really thought that there was something going on in SW other than asset-stripping, padding of accounts and good PR.

He was also trying to go in contradictory directions. On the one hand he was trying to take the unions on board into a tri-

---

[41] Reid p. 71

[42] Geoffrey Howe quoted in Kandiah (ed.) p. 199

[43] Whitehead p. 81. Similar anecdotal evidence is in Campbell p. 526.

[44] Campbell Adamson remembers a dinner at Chequers when the Prime Minister made much of Jim Slater:

'... as if to say to us, the other industrialists, now here is the kind of industrialist I like, he is doing the things you are not doing. He's investing, he's being successful'. Whitehead p. 93.

partite management of the domestic economy; on the other he was attacking them with his industrial relations legislation: on the one hand seeking an investment boom in Britain via cheap credit; on the other unwittingly allowing the introduction of a system which explicitly promised increases in interest rates to 'control' the supply of credit.

In the event, Heath allowed C&CC but would not allow the system to work the way it was supposed to. The theory was that as the money supply expanded, interest rates went up. For political reasons, Heath refused to allow the rates to rise as far and as fast as the monetary experts at the Bank of England wanted.

'The introduction of C&CC was a sign that the cheap credit lobby in Whitehall had been eclipsed. The eclipse was brief. The first serious efforts to allow interest rates to rise after 1971 produced a powerful reassertion of influence by those sensitive to the demands of industrial investors and mortgages in the housing market.'[45]

The result was the worst of all possible worlds; banks printing money day and night with low interest rates. A former senior Bank of England official told Margaret Reid, off the record,

'We little knew that Ted Heath would lose his head and bolt for wildly exorbitant expansion just as C&CC started. The system was meant to rely on interest rate movements and we were going to be allowed to use that instrument as required. Against the background of enormous expansion of the economy with the banks, just released from their shackles, bolting for business, the end result was very different from what we had hoped.'[46]

But blaming Heath, putting the liberation of the banks into the passive voice – the banks released from – and using shackles rather than, say, sensible controls, fails to conceal the Bank of England's role. In their entertaining account of this, Heller and Willatt noted:

'What had been created, under the eyes of the Bank of England, was a simulacrum of the lethally unbalanced Wall Street of the late and roaring twenties... between mid 1970 and early 1974 M3 (currency, current bank accounts and deposit accounts) rose by

[45] Moran (1986) pp. 52 and 3

[46] Reid p. 76

the previously unthinkable amount of 270 per cent... As for the property boom, which would have been impossible without the heavy financing from the banking system, the Bank's sole reaction was a mild directive to the banks in the autumn of 1972, requesting them to make credit less freely available to property companies and for non-industrial purposes.'[47]

William Keegan points out that C&CC became a part of the 'dash for growth' when Chancellor Anthony Barber made bank loans tax deductible for many purposes, including the purchase of homes, second homes and shares – encouraging what was then 'the biggest credit binge in British post-war history'.[48]

How much of the inflation of this period was directly attributable to the activities of the banks is impossible to quantify. In this period there was undoubtedly some wage inflationary pressure coming through from the British trade unions, demand pressure in the domestic economy from the government's increase in the Public Sector Borrowing Requirement in 1972/3 and 1973/4 – not to mention the 1973 increase in the price of oil, rises in other commodities and the rise in food prices resulting from entry into the EEC and membership of the Common Agricultural Policy.[49]

Too late, the government began to realise it had all gone wrong and began to reverse some of the changes made. For a period they even subsidised the building societies to try to prevent the interest rates paid by owner-occupiers from rising above 10%. Incomes policy was reintroduced. In the financial sector, the summer of 1972 saw the Governor of the Bank of England trying informal persuasion, telling the commercial banks that he would not be amused by excessive lending to property speculators. But the pigs were in the trough by then. Eventually the commercial

---

[47] Heller and Willatt, p. 102. Moran gives an amusing account of the various explanations Bank of England officials came up with to explain that the credit explosion signified by the rising money supply figures was not, actually, what it looked like. A decade later Mrs Thatcher was told exactly the same thing by the same officials: the exploding money supply is not what it looks like; the figures are false.

[48] Keegan 1985, pp. 55 and 6. 'Between December 1971 and December 1974 the total assets of British banks rose from £36,865 million to £85,204 million – a rise of £48,339 million or 131 percent.' Printing money with a vengeance! Jay p. 148.

[49] This last point, generally ignored, is made by Douglas Jay p. 155/6.

banks were told to desist from competing with the building societies for the custom of small depositors; and at the end of 1973, with the energy crisis in full swing and the balance of payments deep in deficit, the brakes were slammed on the economy: government spending was cut, surtax was increased, hire purchase controls were reintroduced and the 1971 C&CC reforms were virtually suspended. After 'go' we had returned to 'stop'.

But it was too late – and, for the secondary banking and property sectors, it was too much.[50] The edifice of speculation based on rising property and land prices, began to topple. By early 1974 inflation in Conservative Britain was heading for 20% and the feeding frenzy among the secondary banks led to the Bank of England's secret launching of 'the lifeboat' bearing financial assistance to the stricken money-lenders among the so-called secondary bankers.[51] The bankers had been given their heads and made a mess of it.

---

[50] This view is expressed very strongly by Edward Du Cann, then Chairman of the banker Keyser Ullman in his account of the crisis in his memoir.

[51] Teresa Gorman MP, now one of the 'radical right' group of Tory MPs who supported Mrs Thatcher, first entered politics in 1974, standing as a business-sponsored, independent, anti-Conservative candidate in protest against the Heath government's 20% inflation. Gorman, pp. 162/3.

Chapter Three

1976 And All That

Labour returned to office in February 1974 inheriting the worst trade deficit since the War and record, and still rising inflation. Inflation was not just a British problem, though Britain's inflation was worse than in the other major industrialised nations; and this did not take place in a political vacuum. Most discussions of this period ignore the wider international and the domestic background. On the geopolitical level, the US-dominated post-war order was under unprecedented attack. In South East Asia US power had been defeated, and elsewhere around the US 'empire' there was significant resistance: in Australia, Portugal, Chile, Italy and Angola.[1] Globally, the left seemed to be in the ascendant. This was also true in Britain – the US's partner in the post-war arrangements. The most important problem the US had was in the UK.[2]

A substantial section of the British secret state and its allies in the Conservative Party, business and the media believed, or found it useful to pretend to believe – the distinction is difficult to make – that British democracy, the state, and even the capitalist system were under threat from a resurgent left, spearheaded by the trade unions and manipulated by the British Communist Party under instruction from Moscow. [3] The fact that none of this manifested

[1] For the complete list, and some details see Blum.

[2] The head of the US National Security Council said the British economic crisis 'was considered by us in the White House at that time as the greatest single threat to the stability of the western world.' Fay and Young p. 5

[3] A good example of the theory is the full page article 'Communists Aim to Dictate Labour Policy' in the Daily Telegraph on 28 January, 1974. This period is discussed in detail in Dorril and Ramsay chapters 34-39.

itself via the ballot box – Labour received 37.1% of the votes in the February 1974 election and the Communist Party 0.1% – mattered not.[4] A secret communist conspiracy was, by definition, secret.

Tony Benn was the focus of the anxieties at parliamentary level. In this period he was being surveilled, bugged, wire-tapped, harassed and having his rubbish stolen. MI5 distributed briefings that he had 'contacts in Czech intelligence'.[5] MI5's pretext for this was the fact that Benn, while Minister of Technology, had been lunching with Czech diplomats, some of whom were intelligence officers under cover, and had not reported the contacts to his departmental MI5 officer.[6] But while Benn was the chief focus of the paranoid Right's conspiracy fantasies, the Labour Cabinet was regarded with suspicion generally and many of its members, notably Wilson himself, were subjected to surveillance, burglaries and disinformation in this period. The anti-communist hysteria encompassed the formation of private militias – the so-called private armies – by former intelligence and military personnel, media speculation on the right circumstances for Army intervention in Britain, and a wide range of psy-ops, black bag jobs and disinformation projects running beyond the referendum on Britain's membership of the European Economic Community in 1975.[7]

Just how widely this disinformation about the 'communist threat' had permeated the British state is illustrated by the fact that it had reached Heath's most important civil service ally, Sir Robert Armstrong, the so-called 'Deputy Prime Minister'. In January 1974, at a Ditchley conference, Armstrong harangued the leaders of the CBI about the 'communist threat'.

'We listened to a lecture about how the communists were infiltrating everything. They might even be infiltrating, he said, the

---

[4] Figures from Butler and Kavanagh p. 294.

[5] 'Contacts with Czech intelligence' was next to Benn's name in one of the forgeries made and distributed, using MI5 briefings, by the British Army psy-ops unit in Northern Ireland.

[6] See Dorril and Ramsay ch. 27. While Benn's junior minister at MinTech, John Stonehouse duly obeyed MI5 instructions and reported his contacts with Czech diplomats. MI5 still tried to smear him as a Czech agent.

[7] This period is discussed in detail in Dorril and Ramsay part 4.

room he was in.'[8]

Sean Stewart, in 1975 working for Labour Cabinet member Peter Shore, said:

'I thought the Civil Service was intensely disloyal. Peter Shore was my minister: most of my colleagues thought he was a 'fellow traveller'; and Benn was regarded as a Communist. You would not believe it, would you? In the whole of Whitehall, at the middle level, there was fear all over the place, and the 'antis' [i.e. those anti-EEC membership] were being labelled as Communists and 'fellow travellers'.[9]

Richard Body, a Conservative MP, also then in the 'anti' camp, remembered the same phenomenon:

'There was a great fear being created about the Soviet Union and their allies over here, and there was an inference that those of us in the 'No' side were 'fellow travellers'.[10]

In the year of the referendum, Mrs Thatcher, newly elected leader of the Conservative Party, made her first trip to the United States, where members of her party spread the story of the communist 'threat' to Britain. The late Anthony Verney was then the director of a British firm which made fabrics and was in the United States looking for finance at the time of her visit. He recalled meetings with a representative of the Rockefeller empire which went smoothly until, after the arrival of the Thatcher party in the United States, the banker asked him if it was true that Britain was being run by the communists. The loan did not materialise.[11]

The US took the 1975 referendum on British membership of the EEC seriously enough to send Cord Meyer over to London as temporary CIA Station Chief for the period. Meyer was one of the CIA's most important clandestine operators who had been involved in the manipulation of the youth, student and labour fields in the 1950s and 60s. The news of Meyer's arrival and career, with some documents to back it up, was given to the Conservative MP Richard Body by two CIA officers in London during the referendum campaign. Body was told by these CIA personnel that

---

[8] Campbell Adamson, quoted in Whitehead p. 100.

[9] Broad and Geiger (eds.) p. 103

[10] Ibid.

[11] Verney letter to author.

Meyer had been a well-known federalist in his youth, and was coming over to work for the 'yes' campaign in the referendum.[12] But the mass media in Britain declined to publish the story and it ended up in the then tiny Time Out.[13]

Did it look like a crisis of capitalism? Not really. However, to the US government it did look like a crisis for their post-war economic system. A British rejection of membership of the EEC might have had serious repercussions; as would the introduction of import controls or any other significant deviation from the US economic model.[14] The referendum on British EEC membership was a defining moment of 1970s Britain. The Labour Left and the Tory Right – roughly, the left and right nationalists of British politics – opposed the American-dominated post-war order.[15]

It was a one-sided struggle. The 'yes' campaign had unlimited funding, the support of the City of London, the large British companies, the British state, its broadcasting apparatus (the BBC) and almost all the rest of the media, as well as covert assistance from the CIA and IRD.[16] The 'no' campaign was out-spent ten or fifteen to one. The socialist wing of the Labour Party had made its challenge and been defeated. Prime Minister Harold Wilson immediately removed Tony Benn from his job as Industry

---

[12] Broad and Geiger (eds.) p. 93.

[13] This Time Out story was republished as 'The CIA backs the Common Market' in Agee and Wolf (eds.). I wrote to Sir Richard Body requesting a copy of these documents but did not receive a reply. What Meyer did here, I have no idea; and there is no doubt that the 'Yes' campaign would have won easily without him. Meyer was profiled by Godfrey Hodgson in the Sunday Times Magazine on 15 June 1975, three months after Time Out revealed his arrival. This is reprinted in Agee and Wolf (eds.)

[14] How these consequences were perceived by the US State Department is illustrated below in a long quote from the then US Secretary of State.

[15] Nationalists in economic terms. Tony Benn, for example, would resist to his last breath the claim that he was a nationalist. His grouping on the Labour Left are inclined to describe themselves as 'internationalists' or 'true internationalists', though quite what this means I'm not sure. I discuss this in the concluding chapters.

[16] IRD was the Information Research Department, a clandestine psychological warfare outfit originally created by the Foreign Office in 1947 to engage the Soviet bloc in psy-war. It was shut in 1978. IRD's activities are summarised in Ramsay, 'Clandestine Caucus.'

Minister.

Meanwhile the inflation generated by the Heath Government had reached 27% a year by some accounts and the Wilson Government was perceived by the City-Treasury-Bank of England nexus as not showing sufficient zeal in deflating the economy to reduce it. The financial nexus pushed on two fronts. In 1975 they tried to impose statutory wage controls on the Wilson Government. And failed. In 1976 they tried to impose massive public spending cuts. And failed. Both events contain the same features: demands from the financial sector, political games, and covert operations by sections of the Treasury.

'A VERITABLE CORNUCOPIA OF COINCIDENCE'[17]

To quote Bernard Donoughue,[18] 'Over the final two weeks in June there was a savage and very enjoyable Whitehall battle...' In June 1975 inflation was at 26% or 27%, and, according to Denis Healey who was Chancellor at the time, 'basic hourly rates were up thirty-two per cent on the year'. This was the peak of the inflation mostly generated by the Heath Government[19] – and the peak of the crisis.[20] The Labour Government thought it had an agreement with the Trades Union Congress on wage increases but 'the unions defaulted on their part of the contract,' says Healey: 'A more effective policy for controlling wage increases was now an absolute precondition for saving the economy as a whole'. His memoir gives a brisk and straightforward account of his persuading the Labour Cabinet to accept a statutory incomes policy in early July 1975.[21]

What really happened is much more interesting.

---

[17] Haines p. 59

[18] Donoughue p. 64

[19] I write 'mostly' here because there were other factors involved: rising world commodity prices, notably oil, as well as some wage inflation. It was Heath's misfortune to try and expand the economy and to let the bankers off their leash at precisely the wrong moment. To my knowledge nobody has ever tried to quantify these different inflationary factors.

[20] And it was a real crisis. Inflation at 25% is a crisis for any economic system. Occasionally reading Left accounts of this period you get the impression that this was just a crisis for capitalism.

[21] Healey pp. 394/5.

The key to defeating inflation was then perceived to be through controlling wage increases. Wage costs put up manufacturing costs which were passed on by price rises. But getting a pay rise less than the cost of living increase (inflation) means taking a cut in living standards: this is the nub. How would a government of the urban working class and trade union movement enforce a reduction in the living standards of its constituents? Accepting that it had to be done, Wilson was determined not to make the mistakes the Heath Government had in seeking a pay policy: it would not be legally enforceable, and this time it would include the miners. And getting the miners' approval for such a pay policy, Wilson believed, could only be achieved at the miners' conference in July. The Labour Government was 'playing for time' until July – but under pressure from what Wilson called 'the bailiffs, in the shape of the international financial community, from cautious treasurers of international corporations, multi-nationals, to currency operators and monetary speculators.'[22]

Would they wait for Wilson's 'D-day in the battle against inflation', the miners' annual conference? Bernard – now Lord – Donoughue was then in the Downing Street Policy Unit, and he 'learned from contacts in the Treasury that it had been decided to get the voluntary [pay policy] proposals rejected and to "bounce" a statutory policy through Ministers.'[23] Donoughue informed Wilson of this attempted covert implementation of Treasury policy, and Wilson then:

'... dispatched to the Treasury what is the most commanding document ever sent in British government – a Prime Minister's minute. This... gave blunt instructions not to proceed further with arguments for a statutory policy and to start analysing and constructing a voluntary policy along the lines already supported in [Cabinet committee] MISC 91... *The Treasury ignored the Prime Minister's instructions'*.[24] (Emphasis added.)

On Wednesday 26 June, a speech Wilson proposed to give at

---

[22] Wilson p. 114

[23] Donoughue p. 66 The language of childhood - 'bounce' - is used to partially conceal or underplay what is being described: an unelected group of civil servants trying to impose their views on the government.

[24] Ibid.

the weekend had been circulated through Whitehall: in it he declined to adopt a statutory incomes policy. The speech was going to be delivered on Monday June 30.

'Therefore', says Haines, 'when they went home for the weekend on June 27, 1975, senior officials at the Treasury were not only aware of the Prime Minister's minute to the Chancellor [rejecting a compulsory incomes policy]; they also knew what he intended to say publicly about the prospects for an anti-inflationary policy.'[25]

On Friday the 27th, Wilson predicted to both Joe Haines, his Press Secretary, and Donoughue, head of his Policy Unit, that the governor of the Bank of England or a senior official from the Treasury would appear on Monday, tell him that the pound was about to collapse and that drastic measures needed to be taken.[26]

On Monday 30 June a wave of selling of sterling took place; sterling suffered its biggest fall in a day. The Governor of the Bank of England duly turned up on Monday at 2.45, revealed that sterling was collapsing and urged the Prime Minister to support the Chancellor, Denis Healey, in his proposals for a statutory policy. The inner cabinet committee dealing with this issue, MISC 91, met that evening.

The Treasury policy, presented by Chancellor Healey, was centred round the compulsory incomes policy which for months they had been pressing upon the government and which they had been expressly instructed to abandon by Wilson. Former Chancellor James Callaghan opposed the Treasury advice: he 'had become sceptical of the various predictable kinds of Treasury and Whitehall wisdom'.[27] However, despite his statements earlier in the week, Wilson appeared to be leaning towards a compromise. When Denis Healey saw him earlier that day Wilson ' said he would after all support a statutory pay policy, providing the legal sanctions were directed only against employers who conceded too much, and not against workers who demanded too much'. (Emphasis added.) 28

'At midnight 'as the dinner guests were departing, the

---

[25] Haines p. 52

[26] Haines p. 50, Donoughue p. 66

[27] Donoghue p. 67

[28] Healey p. 94

inevitable Treasury memorandum "bounced" into No. 10. It... contained a totally stark statement of a statutory 10 per cent pay policy, with criminal sanctions.'[29]

Donoughue and Wilson's Press Secretary, Joe Haines, sat down and wrote Wilson a memorandum which began: 'We believe that the Cabinet are being faced with an attempt by the Treasury to stampede it into a statutory pay policy, against every pledge which we have given.'[30]

Joe Haines: 'Bernard Donoughue and I were suspicious about the sudden run on the pound so quickly after the Prime Minister's minute on the previous Friday and his speech at Stoneleigh... There was one further piece of evidence which had come to us during the evening which strengthened our suspicions about the behaviour of the Treasury. No attempt had been made by the Bank of England to keep the pound above the crucial $2.20 level. No money had been spent to bolster the rate... [it was] a veritable cornucopia of coincidence'.[31]

In a rather oblique fashion, Wilson confirmed the Haines/Donoughue account:

'without a legal framework, indeed one backed by criminal sanctions, we [the Cabinet] were told, sterling would go. At 1 a.m. ministers emerging from the Cabinet room were so advised. In this respect Mr. Joe Haines' book reproducing his note to me on the midnight Treasury démarche is accurate.' [32]

But the Treasury/Bank of England manoeuvres failed. The Labour Cabinet did not implement an incomes policy 'backed by criminal sanctions' against employees. And, oddly enough, the pound did not 'go'.

THE IMF INCIDENT

Through the rest of 1975 and into 1976 the situation remained the same. Formally floating, the pound was under constant downwards pressure as a result of British inflation being higher than that of other industrialised countries. Its value was being defended by the Bank of England. Seeking to bring inflation down without

[29] Donoghue p. 68

[30] Haines p. 59

[31] Ibid. pp. 54, 58, 59

[32] Wilson p. 115

a major recession or the massive industrial trouble which had helped end the Heath Government, the Labour Government sought an essentially voluntary incomes policy which would stick. Having failed on the incomes policy front, the Treasury-Bank of England-City nexus sought a reduction in government borrowing and spending. If wages were not going to be cut sufficiently to maintain the pound at the level the financial sector wanted, they would enforce a reduction in consumption of publicly provided goods and services instead. Eventually the government – now led by James Callaghan, after Wilson's resignation – decided to go to the International Monetary Fund to borrow money with which to maintain the value of the pound.

Although it is impossible closely to connect up the two areas, the parapolitical and the financial, the psy-ops campaign against the Wilson Government was still running during this period. The so-called 'private armies' were all funded or run by City figures. The late David Stirling, who had tried to get GB75/Better Britain off the ground, and who by 1976 was working with Truemid, received his funding from the City. The late G.K.Young, who was running the Unison Committee for Action, had been a senior banker after leaving SIS as its no. 2; Unison's members included other City figures, including Anthony Cavendish; and some of General Sir Walter Walker's funding for his Civil Assistance came from the City.[33]

ENTER THE BAILIFFS

'We had the feeling it could really come apart in quite a serious way... so we tended to to see it [the IMF incident] in cosmic terms' – US Secretary of State, William Rogers.

The IMF incident is well documented and hardly needs rehashing here in detail.[34] On one side, the US financial administration, the Conservative Party, most of the media, and some of the Treasury-Bank of England nexus wanted the IMF to impose its traditional policy prescriptions – deflation, in one form or another – as a condition of a loan with which to support the value of sterling. On the other side the Labour Government and some of

---

[33] The details of this are in Dorril and Ramsay ch. 34.

[34] A recent and thorough re-examination is Burk and Cairncross.

the senior Treasury officials wanted the loan but tried to evade, as far as possible, the deflationary conditions which would accompany it.[35] A prolonged game of chicken was played out. Using the prospect of possible economic chaos, damage to NATO - British troop withdrawal from West Germany was talked of at one point – and the threat from the British Left, members of the Labour Cabinet, notably Prime Minister Callaghan and Harold Lever, tried to mobilise political support inside the US government and elsewhere within the NATO alliance against the US Treasury and IMF officials who wished to impose a severely deflationary package on the Labour Government. US Secretary of State at the time, William Rogers, said later of the IMF affair:

'We had the feeling it could really come apart in quite a serious way. As I saw it, it was a choice between Britain remaining in the liberal [i.e. US-dominated] financial system of the West as opposed to a radical change of course, because we were concerned about Tony Benn precipitating a policy decision by Britain to turn its back on the IMF. I think if that had happened the whole system would have begun to come apart. God knows what Italy might have done; then France might have taken a radical change in the same direction. It would not only have had consequences for the economic recovery, it would have had great political consequences. So we tended to see it in cosmic terms.'[36]

RIGGING THE FIGURES

The struggle with the IMF centred round the projected Public Sector Borrowing Requirement (PSBR) – the level of proposed government borrowing. The bigger the projected PSBR, the bigger the cuts the IMF would demand. The Treasury had helped create the sense of crisis six months before, in February 1976, by issuing false figures on public spending which showed that it was taking 60 per cent of Britain's Gross Domestic Product.[37]

---

[35] The leading pro-IMF people identified were Alan Lord and Derek Mitchell at the Treasury and Gordon Richardson at the Bank of England. The 'antis' were Sir Douglas Wass, Permanent Secretary of the Treasury, and Leo Pliatzky. It is generally forgotten that the same forces had used the IMF against the Labour Government in 1969. See Brittan pp. 395 and 6

[36] Fay and Young p. 30

[37] Healey p. 427

Quoting the memoirs of Treasury official at the time, Sir Leo Pliatzky, William Keegan later referred to this false figure as:

'one of the *least fortunate mistakes of the year*, double counting certain items of local authority and nationalised industry spending, and failing to compare like with like, so that what later turned out to be 46 per cent of gross domestic product was printed for all to see as 60 per cent early in that crucial year.'[38] (Emphasis added.)

Only the terminally naive could believe this was a mistake. There had been no previous estimates of the public sector even remotely approaching 60%: the figure must have looked absurd inside the Treasury. This, surely, was just another piece of psychological warfare. The Treasury rigged the figures to make life difficult for the government: by this stage an approach to the IMF was being discussed. A similar move was made during the early stages of negotiations with the IMF. The Treasury's grossly exaggerated estimate of the PSBR for 1977-8 was leaked to The Financial Times.[39]

But with memories of the previous year's Bank of England-led attempt to coerce the Labour Government into a statutory incomes policy, Bernard Donoughue recorded 'suspicions in [the government's] minds that the PSBR had been inflated to create an atmosphere of crisis enabling the Treasury to "bounce" large cuts through Ministers.'[40] These doubts of Donoughue's were not only shared by Prime Minister Callaghan and Cabinet member Peter Shore,[41] the IMF official in charge of the IMF team in London – a former Bank of England official, Alan Whittome – also suspected that the figures had been inflated.[42]

---

[38] The Observer, 21 March 1982

[39] Burk and Cairncross p. 70

[40] Donoughue p. 94.

[41] On 23 November 1976 Tony Benn noted, 'Peter [Shore] suspected the figures produced by the Treasury.' James Callaghan: 'The only doubt in my mind, borne of previous experience, was how far to trust the figures.' Callaghan p. 422

[42] 'Here was evidence that the mandarins were painting a redder picture of the books than the international bankers were. Whose side were they on? Incompetence rather than a deliberate fiddling of the figures is likely to have been the culprit here...' Whitehead p. 192 A great deal about the innocence of British political commentators is expressed in that 'incompetence is likely'.

As it turned out, 'Partly as a result of cash limits, public spending fell sensationally short of expectations in 1976-77, so that the forecasts which so alarmed the IMF and the financial markets painted a much more gloomy picture than was really necessary.[43]

CONSPIRACY

At the time, members of the Callaghan Government knew their opponents were machinating against them. Callaghan 'received well authenticated reports that a prominent front-bench Conservative spokesman, who has since served in Mrs. Thatcher's Cabinet, was in Washington trying to influence the Administration against the Labour Government.'[44] John Par-doe MP in November 1976 stated that 'he had received reliable reports that a number of people from Britain representing both Treasury and City interests had at that time told the US Treasury that it would be better if Britain were to get no more loans from the IMF.'[45] In The Guardian 28 October 1976, Peter Jenkins reported information from a 'wholly authoritative' foreign source (which means a government official):

'One of the problems is the axis between your Treasury and our Treasury. They seem to be agreed that the Labour Manifesto is a manual for suicide... they are in constant touch with our people saying, "Don't bale these bastards out."'[46]

More recently we have learned from Bernard Donoughue that Prime Minister Callaghan, if not the entire Cabinet, knew more than these published fragments suggests. In a 1989 seminar on the IMF incident, Donoughue revealed the following:

'In the middle of this crisis I was privately summoned to the United States Embassy for a secret meeting with a very senior official there who said, "You should be aware of something, which is that parts of the Treasury are in very deep cahoots with parts of the US Treasury and with certain others in Germany who are

[43] William Keegan, The Observer 21 March 1982, citing the memoir by the Treasury official in charge at the time, Sir Leo Pliatzky. Denis Healey wrote in his memoir, 'I cannot help suspecting that Treasury officials deliberately overstated public spending in order to put pressure on governments which were reluctant to cut it.' Healey p. 402

[44] Callaghan p. 43

[45] Coates (ed.) p. 182

[46] Cited in Haines p. 58. This sounds like it came from Donoughue.

of very right-wing inclination and they are absolutely committed to getting the IMF here and if it brings about the break-up of this government, they will be very, very happy." He actually showed me a copy of a secret communication between London and Washington which seemed to confirm this view…'[47]

In his book Prime Minister, Donoughue had earlier written:

'We were not being paranoid in 1976 in our suspicion that the IMF was capable of launching economic "remedies" which would destroy governments (especially governments of the Left). A year later in November 1977 the IMF mission to Portugal (including a senior member of the 1976 mission to the UK) refused to grant a credit tranche to the socialist minority government led by Mr. Soares because he would not make immediate savage economies, which would certainly have brought down his administration and allowed back into power the old anti-democratic parties of the far right. Internal IMF briefing which we saw among diplomatic papers in Downing Street at that time, stated quite brutally that the *IMF policy was to create a foreign exchange crisis over the next two months*. The IMF staff explicitly asked the Western Governments of the United States, Germany, Japan and Britain to withhold financial and economic aid in order to create a foreign exchange crisis which would bring the Soares Government to its knees and so force it to accept the harsh IMF prescription.'[48] (Emphasis added.)

At the end of all the wrangles, the weeks of cabinet debate, the international horse-trading and arm-twisting, and the disinformation from within the financial nexus in Britain, the result was a victory for the Prime Minister. There were three alternatives being considered by the Cabinet. The left, led by Tony Benn, wanted to resist the IMF and introduce a version of the 'siege economy' – import controls and capital controls; in effect, to take Britain out of the international capitalist system. Another group, led by Tony

---

[47] Symposium on the 1976 IMF crisis in Contemporary Record Vol. 3 No. 2 November 1989 p. 43. Donoughue begins this statement with a variation on the standard 'no conspiracy' preamble required in intellectually respectable circles in liberal democracies: 'We all know, and history shows, that most conspiracies were cock-ups. That's the basis I start from.' He then describes a conspiracy, of course.

[48] Donoughue pp. 95/6

Crosland, believed the IMF could not afford to let the British economy fail and thought the government should simply call the IMF's bluff. Accepting the need for a deal with the IMF – if only for the IMF 'seal of approval' to display to the international markets – Callaghan used the NATO alliance dimension to reduce greatly the conditions on the loan. The cuts in public expenditure agreed were smaller than those already working their way through the system as a result of changes inside the Treasury, made before the IMF crisis blew up.

THE LAST BIG 'BOUNCE'

Defeated again, the Treasury faction which wanted the IMF to teach the government a harsh lesson made a final attempt to deceive it. In the Prime Minister's Policy Unit, Bernard Donoughue was monitoring the conclusion of the IMF negotiations. The focus of his interest was the the Letter of Intent, the contract between the government and the IMF:

'It seemed to me very important to scrutinise the small print on this document in case some nasty provisions and unnecessarily harsh conditions had been slipped in at the last moment.'

The Treasury stone-walled him about the Letter of Intent. Eventually he found it in the Prime Minister's box of papers. Donoughue's suspicions were justified:

'The terms were extremely tough, much tougher than had been agreed with the Prime Minister as far as detailed monetary targets were concerned. The imposition of tight ceilings on both the PSBR and on Domestic Credit Expansion (the increase in domestic money supply before making allowance for balance of payments effects) seemed to rule out any possibility of reflation before the next election and even made it likely that we would be forced to trigger off a fresh round of deflationary cuts in order to meet these targets.'

Donoughue claims that with his input Callaghan got significant changes made to the Letter of Intent, notably in raising of monetary ceilings.[49]

In the 1970s Ken Coates was the leader of the Institute for Workers Control, and one of Tony Benn's allies. Now an MEP,

[49] Donoughue pp. 99 and 100 There are other versions of the same events in Whitehead p. 199 and Burk and Cairncross p. 107

Coates is one of those who believed that the Wilson-Callaghan governments of the 1970s betrayed the labour movement and socialism:

'The truth is, Mr. Callaghan had presided over what had been fundamentally, as well as in name, a Liberal-Labour coalition, covering for the International Monetary Fund'[50]

The first part of Coates' statement is true: it was indeed a Lib-Lab pact, fundamentally as well as in name, for a time. But why did Coates think this banality worth prefacing with 'The truth is...'? Who has ever questioned this? And what, if anything, does 'covering for the IMF' mean? After the first 1974 election Labour had only four more seats than the Conservatives and no overall majority. After the second 1974 election there was an overall majority of four which was whittled away by death and by-elections. Between 1974 and 1979 the Labour Party was kept in office by the minor parties, chiefly the Liberals; it received less than 40% of the votes cast in both elections. If Labour did not advance the socialist cause much in the 1970s, it had neither the political power nor the authority – the mandate – to do so. Those on the Labour Left, from Tony Benn down, who believe the Labour Governments of 1974-79 should have and could have acted more radically than they did seem oblivious to these elementary electoral facts. There really was little choice. They did not have the political support in Cabinet, in Parliament, or among the electorate for the radical line offered by the left.

---

[50] Introduction, Coates (ed.) p. 8

Chapter Four

THATCHER'S FIRST GOVERNMENT

In 1976 an unnamed Treasury official was quoted as saying 'we faced the collapse of the currency, the collapse of the government and the collapse of the Labour Party'. The true significance of the 'crisis' in 1976, however, can be judged by the fact that the cuts finally required by the IMF were all quietly restored by the government the following year, only half the IMF loan was used, and the rest was repaid without incident.

Six months after the IMF team flew back to Washington the problem with the pound was not that it was falling too far – the proximate cause of the approach to the IMF in the first place – but rising too fast.

In retrospect, the period between the departure of the IMF team from Heathrow and the Conservative election victory in 1979 is one of the most important in Britain's post-war history: decisions taken and positions adopted in this period determined the direction of British economic policy for 20 years.

However, the contemporary British myth ignores this and sees the period as marked by only three features: the IMF incident, the collapse of the Callaghan Government in the so-called 'Winter of Discontent', and the arrival in 1979 of a Conservative Government led by Margaret Thatcher.

Coming into office in 1979, the so-called monetarist wing of the Tory Party had two basic beliefs about the economy.[1] The first was that the Public Sector Borrowing Requirement (PSBR) caused high interest rates and 'crowded out' private investment. In November 1979 the White Paper, 'The Government's Expenditure

---

[1] Lawson pp. 66 and 7 quotes a paragraph on these beliefs from an article written by him in 1978.

Plans 1980-81', began with the statement, 'Public expenditure is at the heart of Britain's economic difficulties.'[2] Their second belief was that they had to 'control the money supply', in order to control inflation.[3] Where previous governments had believed that wage increases caused inflation and had thus had to wrestle with incomes policy (and the trade unions), Thatcher tells us in her memoir that Enoch Powell:

'had grasped that it was not the unions which caused inflation by pushing up wages, but rather the Government which did so by increasing the supply of money in the economy... incomes policies... leading to strikes which pitted the state against organised labour – were a supreme irrelevance to anti-inflation policy.'[4]

But quite what 'controlling the money supply' meant in practice, they were not too sure.[5] In 1979 the Thatcher-Joseph wing of

---

[2] The supposed relationship between the size of the PSBR and interest rates has been comprehensively falsified. As the first draft was being written in December 1993 the PSBR was around £50 billion and interest rates were around 6%. Conservative MP Jock Bruce-Gardyne MP noted that during 1969/70, the last year of the Wilson Government there was, simultaneously, 'an unprecedented acceleration in unit labour costs coinciding with an equally unprecedented monetary squeeze which the International Monetary Fund had finally imposed on a reluctant Treasury and Bank of England in 1968: in the year to April 1970 the money supply increased by a mere 2.4%.' Bruce-Gardyne p153.

[3] As an undergraduate in the early 1970s I did a subsidiary course in economics. One of the topics was the quantity theory of money – and why it was a joke. It would be hard to exaggerate the contempt in which such beliefs were held by orthodox economists of the period.

[4] Thatcher, Path To Power p141. Given the Heath Government's problems enforcing an incomes policy, the appeal of this nonsense circa 1976 is understandable.

[5] In his memoir Nigel Lawson bemoans 'so little work in Opposition on the conduct of monetary policy'. p17 'Although the Tories in opposition spent a lot of time on drawing up lists of possible cuts in public expenditure, and although they agonised over the perennial no-man's-land topic of trade union reform, monetary policy received little consideration'. Keegan 1985 pp.124-5. See pp.137-9 for discussion. This distinction is all the more interesting for in Keith Joseph's case, his conversion to monetarism was partly a reflection of the experience of the Joseph family firm, Bovis, during the secondary banking boom of 1971/3. Bovis bought a 'fringe' bank which went bust in the slump following the late 1973 boom. 'There was a clear link in Joseph's eyes between the rashness of Bovis's attempt to cash in on secondary banking and the rashness of the Heath Government's dash for growth.' Halcrow p57.

the Conservative Party knew as much about 'controlling the money supply' as the Socialist Workers Party, say, knows about organising a socialist economy. Further, 'controlling the money supply' might look like a surprising ambition for a group of Conservatives. After all, the 'money supply' is primarily the territory of the banks; and the Conservative Party, if it was anything by 1979, was the party of the bankers, the City. How would they 'control the money supply without controlling the money suppliers?[6]

HEATH'S 'MONETARY INCONTINENCE'

The hitherto arcane issue of the money supply got onto the mainstream political agenda in the 1970s because of the Heath Government's famous 'dash for growth' – notably cheap credit and expanding public borrowing and expenditure. This produced both the British economy's traditional balance of payments deficit as imports were sucked in faster than domestic production increased, and increasing inflation for the reasons discussed already. At that point, economic orthodoxy said that domestic consumption should be cut to correct the balance of payments deficit and maintain the external value of sterling. Instead, Heath floated the pound. (President Nixon had already floated the dollar.) Nothing, not even the international value of sterling, was to get in the way.

Before they took office, members of the Thatcher-Joseph wing of the Tory Party had been happy to look part of this reality in the face. Here is a 1978 view of the Heath years from Rhodes Boyson MP, one of the original English nationalist supporters of Mrs Thatcher. Noting the budget deficit generated by the Heath Government and the money supply increases, he commented:

'It was this monetary incontinence (sic) which fanned the flames of the 1973-4 inflation... the true cause of the February 1974 election and the Conservative defeat.'[7]

But Boyson is only looking at half the picture. He blames the

[6] Boyson, 1978, p. 57. This is one of the key texts of Thatcherism in my view, because Boyson, like Mrs Thatcher, saw and expressed things simply and unselfconsciously. Mrs T. also refers to 'monetary incontinence' in her memoirs. See 'The Path to Power' p. 299

[7] Jay p. 149. See also Moran (1986) p. 70

Heath Government for the increase in the money supply, when much of it was generated by the banks themselves. Douglas Jay commented that 'The Private Sector Borrowing Requirement was the trouble'.[8] In the 1980s, not only did the Conservative Party never mention the role of the banks in the great inflation of the 70s, as far as possible they attempted to attribute it to the Labour Government which took office in 1974. Nigel Lawson, for example, writes in his memoir:

'The annual rate of inflation had risen, seemingly inexorably, from 3 per cent under the Conservative governments of 1951 to 1964, to 4 per cent under the first Wilson administration, to 9 per cent under Heath and to 15 per cent under the Labour Government of 1974 to 1979. By the time Margaret Thatcher became the Prime Minister, the British economy was trapped in the cycle of low growth and high inflation which economists called "stagflation"; and mainstream Keynesianism was intellectually and politically bankrupt of solutions to it.'[9]

This is the core of the Tory (and New Labour) counter-revolutionaries' view of 1979 as 'year zero', preceded by a ghastly, Keynesian, quasi-socialist, inflationary nightmare. But on Lawson's own figures, between 1951 and 1966 annual inflation rose from 3 to 4 per cent – one per cent in 15 years – a better record than his monetarily sophisticated, politically correct regime managed in the 1980s, for example. Expressed like this, the unavoidable inference from Lawson's figures is that things started to go wrong in 1970 – when we got a Conservative Government which, among other things, in the name of 'freedom' and 'competition', let the bankers off the leash. By using 'average' inflation rates in this way Lawson is able to present the Heath years as only 'averaging' 9% inflation – concealing the 20% (and

[8] Lawson p. 29.

[9] In her memoir Thatcher acknowledged some of this. Heath, she writes, 'greatly underestimated the stimulating effects of removing credit controls. He felt that emergency fiscal measures were necessary to boost demand and reduce unemployment... Ironically, because it led to higher inflation whose main effects were suffered under the Labour Government, and because inflation destroys jobs rather than preserves them, it ultimately led to higher unemployment as well.' Thatcher, Path to Power p. 213.

rising) which the Labour Government inherited on taking office in February 1974 and began trying to put the Humpty Dumpty of British capitalism back together again.[10] So successful was Chancellor Denis Healey in reining in the banks, that by 1978 Thatcherite Tory MP Rhodes Boyson wrote that 'Denis Healey... could, with some truth, blame the [inflationary] increase on the monetary policy of the previous [Heath] government'; and concludes his account of inflation in the 1970s by talking of 'Labour's monetary restraint', following the fall of the Heath Government.[11]

THE POLITICS OF THE MONEY SUPPLY

Initially, the Tories seem to have assumed that they would 'control the money supply' by continuing with the programme the Labour Government had agreed with the IMF in 1976. Here is Nigel Lawson, Financial Secretary to the Treasury, in charge of monetary policy for the first Conservative Government:

'We assumed too readily that the task was essentially one of applying with conviction the approach that a reluctant Labour Government had had forced upon it by the International Monetary Fund.'[12]

This is a grossly misleading statement. For the IMF's prescription, as agreed in the Letter of Intent from the Callaghan Government to the IMF in 1976, consisted centrally of two things the City did not want: keeping the pound competitive – i.e. cheapish – and the control of Domestic Credit Expansion. The City wanted the opposite: a rising pound and freedom to lend what they wished. As so often, what appears to be a technical, economic question, is actually about power. The period between the IMF visit in 1976 and the return of the Tories in 1979, largely remembered now solely for the 1978/9 'Winter of Discontent', actually contains the key moves which enabled the triumph of the finan-

---

[10] Boyson pp. 58-9. William Keegan points out that 'a table published in the 1982 Medium Term Financial Strategy showed that monetary growth under four years of the "inflationary" Labour Government had averaged 10% (end 1974 to end 1978), whereas from end 1978 to end 1981, the average rate of growth had been 15%.' Keegan 1989, p. 88.

[11] Lawson pp. 17/18

[12] Brittan pp. 165/6, emphasis added.

cial sector under Thatcher and Lawson to take place; and the most important move of all was the abandoning of the IMF's Domestic Credit Expansion and its replacement as key indicator of the money supply by sterling M3.

Domestic Credit Expansion (DCE) was first introduced into British economic life by IMF officials in October 1968 at the time of the Wilson Government's approach to the IMF for financial assistance. Samuel Brittan can explain:

'[DCE] is based on the fact that an expansion of bank credit to the public or private sector automatically increased money supply in ordinary circumstances... It is the total 'credit' extended to the British economy from all sources. This is defined in 'Financial Statistics' as the sum of domestic bank lending to the public and private sectors and the overseas financing of the public sector, plus one or two adjustments. Looked at this way the definition of 'credit', which excluded credit supplied outside the banking system, but includes long-term overseas lending to nationalised industries, seems very arbitrary.

'It is much more helpful to look at the liabilities side. This gives an alternative, but equivalent, definition of DCE as the increase of the money supply plus the payments deficit (or minus the surplus). Looked at this way a DCE limit, such as the £400m ceiling imposed for 1969-70 under IMF influence, *limits the permissible growth of the money supply according to the balance of payments.* If this is in surplus, the money supply can grow more than the DCE limit. If this is in deficit it cannot grow as much and, if the deficit is large enough, it may even have to fall.'[13]

This was then the standard IMF position. Their primary aim with countries has always been to achieve balance of payments equilibrium, usually by depressing domestic consumption. Hence the linking of DCE – and thus domestic consumption – to the balance of payments position. If the position is poor, and the economy is running a balance of payments deficit, domestic credit expansion – i.e. domestic economic activity – is reduced. For the Labour Government of 1976 the IMF 'had insisted on setting monetary targets... Domestic Credit Expansion... was to be progressively reduced from £9 billion in 1976-77 to £7.7 billion in 1977-78 to £6 billion in 1978-9. It was also expected that the

[13] Burk and Cairncross p. 107

increase in M3 would be be between 9 and 13 per cent.' (Emphasis added.)[14] Please note: in their agreement with the Labour Government, the IMF had not wanted the economy run according to sterling M3; it was just going to be another, secondary indicator. You might think running the economy along the lines suggested by Domestic Credit Expansion would suit a traditionally deflation-inclined Treasury. However, controlling Domestic Credit Expansion is achieved by government restrictions on the generation of credit by the banking system. This was not what the City wanted. Brittan notes (p. 167):

'considerable doubts did, however, develop about DCE in the British Treasury as its implications were closely examined. For DCE purposes the balance of payments surplus included *overseas* lending to the private sector, on long-and short-term capital account; and officials were naturally reluctant to see the money supply tied too closely to this *volatile* item.' (Emphasis added.)

And if the Treasury did not like DCE because it was 'arbitrary' and 'volatile', the banks did not like it because it linked domestic credit expansion – essentially bank lending – with activities which included overseas lending by the banks themselves.

In effect, DCE meant the more lent overseas, the less could be lent in the UK; which, in turn, implied controls over bank lending – and this went against all the City's attempts, since the early 1950s, to obtain 'freedom' for their activities. Domestic Credit Expansion as the primary expression of monetary growth in the UK economy was acceptable to no-one in the financial nexus. So the Treasury and Bank of England chose the other, secondary indicator of money supply indicated by the IMF, sterling M3, as its guiding light.

Quite how this manoeuvre was achieved has not been explained: none of the commentators on the period, including Chancellor Healey himself, discuss this. Since sterling M3 had always been the monetary indicator of choice for the Treasury and Bank of England, reinstating it as primary indicator was back to business as usual. And the change was critical. For while the British economy continued to meet the targets for Domestic Credit Expansion agreed with the IMF, sterling M3 expanded too far.

---

[14] Quoted in David Smith p. 68.

GOODBYE TO THE IMF

The twin IMF prescriptions for the economy, keeping the pound competitive and steering the money supply by Domestic Credit Expansion figures were abandoned in 1977. Attempting to keep the pound competitive, interest rates were reduced as low as 5% – giving negative real interest rates at the bottom of the credit chain. Despite this the pound continued to rise as speculators saw sterling as a good bet, (a) because of the IMF's 'seal of approval' and (b) because of Britain's position as an oil producer in the near future.

At that point a range of options were available to stop the currency rising but they all involved severe controls over the flows of speculative money coming into London. These kinds of controls were apparently not considered. The Bank of England, however, saw an opportunity to get rid of exchange controls: the idea being that the 'hot' money coming into London would be balanced by UK money going abroad. But this option was rejected by the Labour Cabinet. At this point somehow the government was persuaded that the best alternative was to allow the pound to rise. On 31 October 1977 the Treasury announced that it was abandoning its policy of trying to keep the pound 'competitive' and was letting the pound rise because:

'A continuance of foreign inflows on a large scale could endanger continued adherence to the domestic monetary targets.'[15]

These 'domestic monetary targets' were sterling M3, not Domestic Credit Expansion, which remained well within the IMF's suggested targets.[16] 'Monetarism' in Britain, the sacrifice of the real economy to meet notional financial targets, which expressed – and disguised – the interests of the financial sector, begins here.[17]

Referring to the 1978 period when Chancellor Healey first began to be driven by sterling M3, Bryan Gould commented:

'The City liked sterling M3 because it was a figure which was entirely under their control. If they chose to buy gilts [govern-

---

[15] Ibid. p. 69

[16] In his memoir Healey tried to finesse his way past this - and fails, in my view. See Healey p. 435. The truth is he did not realise what the game was at this point.

[17] Gould p. 127

ment debt], the figure would be low. If they chose not to, the figure would rise and would signal the need to tighten monetary policy. [i.e. put interest rates up]. The money markets therefore exercised total control over economic policy on a month-by-month basis. The City decided that the 1978 budget was a bit too expansionary for their liking and that they would need higher rates of interest before they would buy gilts. When they therefore held off for a month and the sterling M3 figures duly rose, Healey had no option but to raise interest rates, thereby choking off the modest expansion he had planned.'[18]

The Treasury welcomed so-called 'monetarism' not because they believed the crude theories about the supposed relationship between the money supply and inflation, but because in the form that monetarism was being being considered in the early years of the Thatcher Government, that is trying to meet targets for sterling M3, 'it provided a direct bridge to the government's [and Treasury's] other ambition – to shrink the size of the state and lower taxes by cutting public spending and borrowing'.[19] The public sector borrowing requirement (PSBR) – the gap between government spending and revenues from taxation – was included in sterling M3, the indicator of money adopted as the key one by the government.

'Reducing public borrowing was integral to controlling the government's chosen measure of money. Douglas Wass, the permanent secretary, and other senior officials did not share Lawson's monetarist zeal but they recognised the potential advantage of a policy which promised clarity and simplicity. The message to the cabinet was unequivocal: unless it reined back spending, the growth rate of sterling M3 would overshoot its targets... Monetarism, as one senior official put it "provided just the right structure of incentives... we never really believed in sterling M3, but it was helpful that ministers did."'[20]

NORTH SEA OIL

And then there was North Sea oil. From 1975 onwards, after

[18] Philip Stephens p. 12

[19] Ibid.

[20] See 'Banks To Get Tax Relief On Bad Overseas Loans' in The Guardian, 21 January, 1983.

inflation, the prospect of North Sea oil revenues was the biggest item on the agenda of the UK economy. There are essentially two economies in the UK. One is the domestic, manufacturing economy and its allied services; the other consists of the City of London, its support services in the ring of shires round the capital, and some multinationals with bases and plant in the UK. The dominance of the southern, City-based, overseas-oriented economy in the 1980s could hardly have been more obvious.

Manufacturing output fell by about 25% and the City boomed. House building plummeted, thousands slept on the streets, and billions were invested in the City's expansion into dockland. The banks made so much money in the early 1980s that even the Tories eventually levied a notional 'windfall tax' on them – though it was more than compensated for by tax allowances on bad overseas loans announced in 1983.[21]

The extent of the financial sector's dominance can be demonstrated most vividly by trying to imagine a Britain in which the City declines by 20% and manufacturing is doing so well a 'windfall profits' tax has to be levied on it...

Rooted in the trade unions, and thus in the domestic manufacturing economy, in the late 1970s the Labour Party saw the forthcoming oil revenues, at a minimum, as representing freedom from the constraints of balance of payments deficits generated when previous post-war governments (Macmillan, Wilson, Heath) had tried to expand the domestic, manufacturing economy.[22]

But the financial sector and the Tory Party had other ideas. Rather than have the oil wealth invested in the UK, in manufacturing or infrastructure developments, the City wanted to use it to recreate the its pre-war role of financier to the world; and, curiously, by 1977 the Conservative Party's shadow spokesmen were all beginning to sing a similar song about the forthcoming oil revenues – a song they were learning from the City of London.

The economist Gordon Pepper, then the monetary expert at the City firm of Greenwells, and as Nigel Lawson tells us, a man

---

[21] Quite what Labour would have done with the oil revenues had they won the election of 1979 is unclear to me.

[22] On becoming leader of the Conservative Party, Mrs Thatcher was tutored in economics by a group of monetarists, including Alan Walters, Brian Griffiths, Pepper and Samuel Brittan. Thatcher, Path to Power, p. 303.

with Mrs Thatcher's ear,[23] edited a Special Monetary Bulletin, published by Greenwells. In the edition of 1 July 1977, 'The Economic Implications of North Sea Oil', Pepper concluded that sterling should be allowed to float freely and exchange controls should be relaxed, allowing the oil revenues coming in to be balanced by capital exports going out. He argued thus: if revenues build up, the balance of payments surplus will lead to pressure on the money supply, leading to faster inflation and lower growth. He concluded:

'If the authorities do not intervene heavily in the foreign markets and resist an appreciation of the pound then North Sea oil will have a beneficial effect on the economy. If... they continue their present policy of intervention to push the [sterling] rate down, monetary growth will tend to be excessive and will damage growth.'

In one neat little package, concern about monetary growth produces the abolition of exchange controls (old money out to balance new oil money in), and an appreciating pound – the two things the City needed. But Pepper says not a word about the effects of the domestic manufacturing economy of an appreciating pound.

In a speech in the same month, July 1977, Shadow Chancellor Geoffrey Howe did consider the position of the manufacturing economy, claiming that scrapping exchange controls would prevent the pound rising too far and damaging manufacturing.[24] On 27 August The Times reported Shadow Cabinet member Leon Brittan stating that 'the best use the UK could make of the economic benefits of North Sea oil would be to let the pound rise in a genuinely free float'; on 29 October it reported shadow Treasury minister David Howell advocating a 'strong pound'; and on 1 November it reported Shadow Chancellor Geoffrey Howe claiming that 'Relaxation [of exchange controls] would also prevent the pound from rising *artificially* high and damaging the competitiveness of our exports... [and] would boost overseas investment and *increase opportunities* to improve Britain's invisible exports.' (Emphases added.)[25]

---

[23] Quoted in Riddell p. 34.

[24] The general tenor of the oil debate can be seen at a glance in The Times Index for 1977, especially p. 375, under Economic Situation and Policy.

'DEINDUSTRIALISATION IS GOOD FOR THE UK'

The idea that the oil revenues would raise the value of the currency and thus damage manufacturing was taken up in the economics media. On 26 November 1977, The Economist discussed the so-called 'Dutch disease', the experience of the Dutch economy in the early 1970s when gas from the North Sea hit the Dutch economy. The resulting reduction in energy imports caused a trade surplus, and a rise in the value of the guilder.

This made Dutch exports more expensive and imports cheaper. This argument was put by Hugh Stephenson in The Times in the same month, again concluding that the 'Dutch disease' could be avoided by lifting exchange controls.[26] For the most influential financial journalist of the period, Samuel Brittan, scrapping exchange controls was the 'only serious way of preventing North Sea oil from imposing a contraction in manufacturing...'[27]

This was all very well – and might have worked; we'll never know. On paper, anyway, if wealth going out is balanced by wealth coming in, the effect on the exchange rate should be zero. But while Pepper, explicitly, and Shadow Chancellor Howe, implicitly, expected oil to push up the value of the pound,[28] no-one in this period seems to have included in their speculations that the government would raise interest rates to 'control' the money supply on top of the appreciation expected to arise from its status as a 'petro-currency'. Frank Blackaby noted during the great appreciation of the pound in 1980, that while the government hoped that a substantially increased capital outflow would help

[25] Hugh Stephenson, 7 November, 1977.

[26] The Financial Times, July 3 1980. Brittan's piece was headed, 'Deindustrialisation is good for the UK'. The same view was expressed by Roy Peters in 'Overseas Portfolio Investment – Developments Since the Abolition of Exchange Controls', in the NatWest Quarterly Review, May 1981: 'It may be that the only way to protect manufacturing industry in the short term is to ensure that there are sufficient outflows on the capital account to stop sterling rising further.' There are, of course, other ways to prevent a currency appreciating, of which maintaining extremely low interest rates is the the most frequently used. Japan followed this course for decades.

[27] Howe spoke the danger of the pound 'rising artificially high'. By inference, a 'natural' rise would be acceptable.

[28] Frank Blackaby, 'Exchange-rate Policy and Economic Strategy' in Three Banks Review, June 1980.

to keep the exchange rate down, it did not happen:

'Far from *discouraging* capital inflows, the government — pursuing a high interest-rate policy in the interests of its money supply target – has *encouraged* them.'[29] (Emphases added.)

The abolition of exchange controls and a government willing to impose high interest rates 'to control the money supply' produced what Tom Nairn described as 'dream conditions for London's financial apparatus in 1980 and 1981'.[30]

SETTING THE MONEY-LENDERS LOOSE

Controlling the money supply was only one item on the Lawson-Howe agenda – and the secondary one, at that. First came abolishing exchange controls and the other restrictions on the financial sectors' activities. On 4 October 1979 Nigel Lawson minuted Chancellor Howe advocating complete abolition of exchange controls and this was announced by Howe, after passing it through Cabinet, on 23 October.[31] Unconcerned by the mess created by partial deregulation of the financial sector between 1971 and 1974, between 1979 and 1982 the government:

- abolished exchange controls;
- ended the restrictions on building society lending – starting them off on the road to becoming banks – and thus beginning the great credit explosion of the later 1980s;
- abolished the so-called 'corset', the restrictions on bank lending which had been introduced by the previous government;
- abolished the Reserve Assets Ratio which made the banks hold at least 12.5% of their deposits in some specified range of liquid assets;
- and abolished hire-purchase restrictions.[32]

At the top of this City shopping list was the abolition of exchange controls. Among the lobby for their abolition were

[29] Nairn p. 392

[30] Lawson p. 40 Lawson notes there was only one voice in Cabinet raised against it - Michael Heseltine, who argued that people would abuse their freedom and invest in villas in France not in Britain. That was the point, Michael.

[31] These measures are proudly listed by Nigel Lawson in his memoir on p. 626.

[32] Lawson p. 39

'most of the top people at the Bank of England, especially those responsible for administering exchange controls', [33] Nigel Lawson [34] – and Mrs Thatcher, who tells us in her memoir that she 'took greatest personal pleasure in [their] removal.'[35]

The result of the abolition of exchange controls was visible almost immediately: capital hitherto invested in the UK began going abroad. In the Guardian of 21 September, 1981, Victor Keegan noted:

'Figures published last week by the Bank of England show that pension funds are now investing 25% of their money abroad (compared with almost nothing a few years ago) and there has been no investment at all (net) by unit trusts in the UK since exchange controls were abolished.'

But this dose of 'freedom' for the financial sector, what Nigel Lawson calls 'liberalisation', made a nonsense of the Thatcher government's stated desire to 'control' the money supply. As Lawson himself notes in his memoir (p. 72), scrapping exchange controls meant that 'money aggregates [became] more difficult to predict and control.' For 'more difficult' read impossible. Shortly after this he states: 'If inflation is to be squeezed, money has to become more difficult to borrow. And in a liberalised system that must mean paying a higher price for it.' (p. 76) Lawson conflates money becoming more difficult to borrow with money becoming more expensive to borrow. But having scrapped all the controls over the amount of money the banks could lend, he does not have much choice. The problem for the Tories, qua party of the City, of how to control the money supply without

---

[33] On page 41 of his memoirs Lawson tells us that without the abolition of exchange controls, 'the City would have been hard put to remain a world-class financial centre.'

[34] The Downing Street Years p. 44. Lawson 'had no doubt that, with sterling buoyed up by the combination of its petro-currency status and growing international confidence in the sound monetary policies of the new Government - whatever they might turn out to be! - early and complete abolition was not only achievable but economically necessary.' (Lawson p. 39)
My sister keeps reminding me that Mrs Thatcher was married to a director of an oil company and must have been getting at least some of her economic ideas from him.

35 Guardian, 2 September, 1983, 'UK's overseas assets jump to £42.4 billion'. These figures are a tribute to the efficacy of exchange controls.

controlling the money suppliers, was solved by scrapping the controls over the banks, giving the money suppliers their heads – and then insisting that they charge very high interest rates on the loans! This was the rebirth of the C&CC changes of 1971, with the addition of the abolition of exchange controls sought by the creators of Operation Robot in 1952. It had been nearly 30 years since Robot had been rejected but finally the City was free from government restrictions.

Chapter Five

SEEKING A WAY OUT

The beauty of the simple-minded 'monetarism' which the Thatcher government espoused in 1979 and 1980 was the way it justified putting up and keeping up interest rates until sterling M3 behaved in the way predicted by the theories. Throughout 1980, as sterling M3 refused to fall far enough, the value of the pound appreciated – eventually up to $2.40, the level it had been in 1967 – and British manufacturing slumped and collapsed. Oil provided a convenient explanation for that rise in sterling. A headline in the Sunday Times Business News of July 20, 1980 (p. 56), proclaimed, 'How North Sea oil is killing our industry'. This thesis reached some kind of apotheosis the following year in R. J. Forsyth and J. A. Kay's 'Oil Revenues and Manufacturing Output', in which '[a] contraction of manufacturing output and an increase in the domestic absorption of imported manufactures' had become 'the *only means* by which the British economy can benefit from the North Sea.'[1] (Emphasis added.)

So, in the end, the financial experts concluded, there was no alternative: oil was bound to push up the value of sterling because oil-backed currencies are attractive to foreign capital. The rise in the value of sterling between 1979 and 1981, which destroyed a quarter of British manufacturing industry, was merely the mechanism through which the balance of trade between this country and the rest of the world corrected itself. When we had to import large quantities of oil, a large proportion of manufacturing output was needed to pay for it. Importing no oil, we needed less manu-

[1] Fiscal Studies, July 1981. Quite how a contracting manufacturing base and increasing imports benefited the UK is not explained.

facturing output.[2] Had we attempted to maintain the pre-oil volumes of manufacturing output, our economy would have run a huge trade surplus and that would have pushed up the value of sterling even further. In 1978, we learn from Frank Blackaby:

'a senior Treasury official laconically remarked, "Perhaps we can either have North Sea oil or manufacturing industry, but not both."'[3]

What he really meant was: we can have two of the following: the City, manufacturing, or North Sea oil. But it would never have occurred to him to consider not having the City.

And so, in this best of all possible worlds, far from being a bad thing, the massive flight of capital from this country between '79 and '83 was a good thing. It helped to balance the capital inflows from the North Sea, preventing an even bigger trade surplus and the destruction of more British manufacturing! It was this situation which led former senior Treasury official Leo Pliatzky, intending no irony, to write that,

'It is understandable that people are frustrated that more primitive (sic) countries which produce oil have used the revenues from it to finance industrial and social development while in Britain both have been cut back since the North Sea oil came on stream.'[4]

Indeed.

The theory followed the money. In fact all that happened is that economic policy followed the money. Frank Blackaby noted in 1980:

'just at the time when oil output was building up, there was a major swing in fashion in thinking about the exchange rate. Up to 1977, the doctrine had been to use the exchange rate to preserve competitiveness – indeed, this principle was written into the first letter of intent at the time of the 1976 IMF loan. The doctrine was then changed to assert that (a) there should be no exchange-rate

---

[2] Hamish MacRae in the Guardian, October 13, 1981: 'As the energy sector grows, something has to shrink.' In this curious universe it is unclear how countries ever get richer, for as one sector grows, another, apparently, has to shrink. Did the Saudis grow fewer dates?

[3] Frank Blackaby, 'Exchange Rate Policy and Economic Strategy' in Three Banks Review, June 1980.

[4] Pliatzky p. 194

policy, and (b) that a high exchange rate was a *good thing*.' (Emphasis added.)

Blackaby called this 'one of those unfortunate accidents which have so bedevilled British economic policy since the war'.[5] (Emphasis added.) In the same year, coming from a similar liberal-Keynesian position, the Guardian's Victor Keegan asked:

'What happened to the oil revenues which, five years ago, led people to expect the dawning of a new age of prosperity? Most of it, in the *supreme irony of economic history*, has gone to pay out unemployment to those who would not have lost their jobs if we had not discovered it in the first place.'[6] (Emphasis added.)

But of course 'the doctrine' on exchange rate policy changed in 1977 with the dawning of oil revenues. These 'ironies' and 'accidents' always work in the same direction – in the interests of the City, not the manufacturing economy – and have done so since the restoration of the gold standard. Nothing was more certain, for example, than that Britain would join the ERM at too high a sterling value for the manufacturing sector. 'Twas ever thus.

The London financial elite had always wanted a high sterling exchange rate: it attracts other peoples' money to London (they make money handling money), and it has other profitable consequences. It enables them to force up domestic interest rates, 'to control inflation'. (If the exchange rate is low, interest rates are put up 'to defend the value of the currency'.) And with high interest rates domestic loans pay more. It is a wonderful system; and, yes, it is precisely the racket it appears.

The policy and the theory follows the money. That is all there is to it. There has never been a clearer illustration of economics as ideology. To some commentators outside the UK, and independent of the influence of the City's interests, it looked rather different. In 1981 the Norwegian economist Oystein Noreng wrote that the Tories' monetarism could be seen 'as a deliberate policy of keeping the petroleum revenues outside the UK domestic economic circuit and preventing them from benefiting UK manufacturers in the form of increasing access to capital.'[7]

---

[5] Blackaby op. cit.

[6] Victor Keegan, Guardian, 16 May 1983

[7] 'Petroleum Revenues and Industrial Income', Oystein Noreng, in Barker and Brailovsky (eds) p. 232.

This was precisely what Gordon Pepper had recommended in 1978, as quoted in the previous chapter, though Pepper framed it in terms of keeping the revenues from inflating the money supply.

In the Thatcher period the City was given its head. Exchange controls were abolished, interest rates jacked up and almost all of the remaining financial controls were scrapped. Accompanying this was the elaborate charade of 'self regulation' – i.e. non regulation – the ultimate expression of the City's independence from the rest of British civil society. The result was the 'loadsamoney' culture in the 1980s, and the fantasies being put out about by the City, parts of the Treasury and Bank of England, that Britain was on some natural evolutionary path towards becoming a post-manufacturing or post-industrial service economy.[8] Nigel Lawson contemptuously offered this line in 1985 to a House of Lords committee looking at Britain's shrinking manufacturing base.

It did not matter that Britain was making fewer and fewer products: they would be replaced by more and more 'financial products' (a term which came into use in the mid-1980s, as the language, like the economic theory, also followed the money). This was accompanied by the expansion of the City's cultural hegemony out from the financial pages of the non-tabloid newspapers into the mass media, as all-purpose, self-serving, experts on everything.

Former Treasury mandarin, Leo Pliatzky:

'It was a strange period to look back on. There appeared to be a great gulf between attitudes in much of the City and in industry throughout the country. In some quarters there was a Khomeni-like fanaticism abroad, a reluctance to see the connection between high interest rates and a crippling exchange rate. North Sea oil had made sterling a petro-currency, it was alleged; the days of manufacturing were over.'[9]

Mrs Thatcher also bought this line for a while. In his memoir the former BBC political correspondent, John Cole, describes asking Mrs Thatcher for an example of how this 'service' or 'post-

---

[8] Lawson appears to believe that as oil revenues decline, manufacturing, wrecked in the 1980s, will spontaneously regenerate itself! See Lawson pp. 195 and 6. Not so far, Nigel.

[9] Pliatzky p. 128

industrial economy' would work:

'She cited an entrepreneur she had met the previous week, who wished to take over Battersea power station and turn it into what we both then knew as a "Disneyland", but subsequently learned to call a theme park.'

The next day Cole recounted this to the Economic Attaché of the United States embassy.

'He looked at me in genuine astonishment, thoughtfully laid down his fork, and exclaimed: "But gee, John, you can't all make a living opening doors for each other."'[10]

The Reagan/Thatcher period was marked by colossal, officially sanctioned 'rip-offs' of the collective by groups of individuals. In the US this was done through the 'looting' of local banks, the so-called Savings and Loans, and the use of taxes to pay for the expanding arms industries. In Britain, the money has been made through the consequences of privatisation – the conversion of the (savings) taxes of the many to the property of the few; through the privatisation process – sell-offs organised by City merchant banks, making hundreds of millions in fees; fees which the government refuses to disclose on grounds of 'commercial confidentiality';[11] and as consultants and experts, 'advising' the public sector. This last parasitic activity on the remnants of the British state reached an absurd climax with the news in March 1994 that the Department of Social Security had paid out more than £100 million in management fees in 1993 – while only giving £97 million in grants to the poor.[12]

How well Mrs Thatcher understood any of this is not clear. Having told us in her memoirs how proud she was to have been associated with the abolition of exchange controls, she spends the next hundred pages intermittently complaining about the level of interest rates her government had imposed. It is clear that

[10] Cole p. 209

[11] What did privatising a public utility amount to? Write, print and distribute a brochure; make a guess at a price per share, always on the low side so the shares will sell; print a lot of application forms; pay for some TV and newspaper adverts; send out the brochures; collate the names and addresses of the buyers; collect X million pounds as your fee. I think Hull City Council's Housing Benefit Office could do it given a few extra staff. One of the great rip-offs of the 20th century.

[12] Observer, 27 March, 1994, 'City Advice cost DSS £100 million'.

like the other 'monetarists' in her government, Mrs Thatcher did not really know much about 'controlling the money supply' - or, indeed, about what 'the money supply' was - and seems to have assumed it could be done relatively easily and quickly. When she saw that it could not, and what the consequences were for the domestic economy of the regime of high interest rates apparently necessary to 'control' the money supply, she began looking for a way out.

As Nigel Lawson keeps reminding readers in his memoir, Mrs Thatcher did not like what you had to do to get inflation down under a 'liberalised' system. The veritable 'Countess of Soundmoney', Mrs Thatcher was among those who did not accept, as Lawson did, that the only way to 'control' the money supply was by using high interest rates to depress the domestic economy. Lawson sneers in his memoirs that:

'there was no more assiduous seeker for gimmicks which would supposedly give us tight money without high interest rates than Margaret Thatcher.'[13]

In fact, he only mentions one such 'gimmick', something called Monetary Base Control; which, instead of trying to influence the demand for money via interest rates, tries to control the supply of money more directly by setting a target for the banks' reserves with the Bank of England; in other words, by trying to control the amount of money the banks could lend.[14]

There are striking parallels between the experience of Thatcher and Heath. Both took office believing they knew how to combat the 'British disease'; both were primarily interested in the domestic economy. The agenda of 'Selsdon man' and that of Thatcherism were pretty similar: reduce union power and public spending; give the economy a bracing dose of 'freedom' and market forces; reduce the state's role in the economy. Yet both of them came a-cropper at the hands of the City.

In 1970, not understanding British capitalism, Heath was

[13] p. 77

[14] On MBC, for example, see the discussion in Llewelyn (ed), pp. 56-60; Lawson pp. 80 and 81 for his reasons for rejecting it. Milton Friedman, the guru of monetarism: 'Direct control of the monetary base is an alternative to fiscal policy [i.e. taxes] and interest rates as a means of controlling monetary growth.' (Emphasis added.) Cited in David Smith p. 95. Direct control was precisely what the City wanted to avoid.

ambushed by the financial sector, in the shape of the Bank of England, and was persuaded to let the banks off the leash – with disastrous consequences - while thinking he was doing something else. Heath eventually regained some control of the banks, but not before immense damage was done. In response to Heath's 'monetary incontinence', and coached in the 1970s by a group of monetarist economists, including Alan Walters and Gordon Pepper, Mrs Thatcher had thought she was elected to 'control the money supply', to 'restore honest or sound money'.

It would be difficult to exaggerate the significance of this to Mrs Thatcher at this time. She even seems to have recognised what went wrong. In her memoir she wrote that Heath 'greatly underestimated the stimulating effects of removing credit controls.'[15] Yet in 1979 Mrs Thatcher was persuaded to remove the rest of the controls on the financial sector - with even more disastrous consequences. But where Heath succeeded in stuffing part of the genie back in the bottle Mrs Thatcher failed - but not without a struggle. Thanks to the Thatcher and Lawson memoirs, we now can recreate that struggle between Mrs Thatcher and her advisers, mostly from the Centre for Policy Studies, on the one side, and the Treasury and Bank of England – and their political front-men, Lawson and Howe – on the other.[16]

THATCHER VERSUS THE TREASURY MINISTERS

In October 1979 Chancellor Geoffrey Howe announced the end of the remaining exchange controls (some had been scrapped in June). The next month the Thatcher government raised interest rates to a minimum 17% – nearer 30% for most individual customers – where they stayed for eight months. The pound soared in value as 'hot money' poured into London attracted by real interest rates of over 5%.[17] British exporters and manufacturers began to collapse but the champagne began to flow in the boardrooms of the banks. No exchange controls, no limits on lend-

[15] Path to Power p. 217

[16] On line five of the first page of his memoir, Lawson tells us that his father was 'the proprietor of a small but successful firm in the City of London.' Lawson was the quintessential 'City man'.

[17] The 'real' interest rate is the stated interest rate minus inflation. 17% interest rate with 12% inflation is a real interest rate of 5%. In the 1930s real interest rates were 3% or less.

ing, and record interest rates - this was everything the City had been seeking to recreate since the end of World War 2 – and more. But the money supply did not behave as it should have. By the end of the first year in office Mrs Thatcher was facing the failure of one of her central policies – and the falsification of one of her central economic beliefs. Just like Heath, she questioned the policies they had implemented and she began looking for a way out.

Against the alliance of City interests seeking to retain their 'freedom' led by Howe and Lawson, lined up Mrs Thatcher and a group of unofficial advisors – economists such as Brian Griffiths, Gordon Pepper and Alan Walters – who urged the adoption of control of the monetary base (MBC) as the better method of 'controlling the money supply'.[18] The editor of monetary bulletins published by Greenwells, the stockbrokers, Pepper was one of the first within the City to express concern at the growth of the money supply in the 1970s.[19] Pepper, who seems to have taken 'controlling the money supply' seriously,

'had established a private line to Margaret Thatcher when she was Leader of the Opposition... [and] persuaded her that a given degree of monetary tightness could, through MBC (monetary base control), be secured at an appreciably lower level of interest rates than the UK was experiencing. Given her – by no means unique – detestation of high interest rates, a promise of sufficient monetary tightness to bring down inflation at lower interest rates had an irresistible appeal.'[20]

But the newly liberated financial system would not have it. Nigel Lawson tells us that the Bank of England 'deeply disliked the whole idea of MBC,' and he 'was convinced that such an experiment had a chance of success only if those responsible for its implementation wished to make it a success. Given the Bank's profound antipathy, it would all too likely have proved the disaster they predicted.'[21] In other words, the Bank was not under political control, and would make MBC fail. And Mrs Thatcher

[18] Thatcher Path to Power, pp. 133 and 4

[19] Keegan 1985 p. 41

[20] Lawson pp. 79 and 80

[21] Ibid. pp. 80 and 81 'The idea [of MBC] was always repugnant to the Bank of England – which takes its primary function of being "lender of last resort", to the banking system more seriously than the achievement of any quantitative target.' Keegan 1989, p. 69.

tells us that, 'the Treasury were not prepared to move to the system of monetary base control which Alan [Walters] favoured and to which I was attracted by his clear and persuasive analysis.'[22] Philip Stephens tells us that the Treasury was hostile to MBC because 'it wanted to retain the link between money and public borrowing provided by sterling M3.'[23] In other words, the Treasury regarded controlling public spending as more important than controlling the money supply. Mrs Thatcher got the Treasury's consolation prize: 'Bank of England and Treasury officials *were instructed* to put together proposals for changing the methods of monetary control, with a view to moving away from excessive reliance on high interest rates.'[24] (Emphasis added.) 'Action this day' it was not.

The Bank of England and Treasury proposals on monetary control were published in March 1980 as a so-called 'green paper' – a discussion document – which 'stopped well short of a move towards a monetary base system'.[25] While sterling M3 was to remain the guiding light of policy, changes in methods 'consistent with the eventual adoption of a monetary base system' were also introduced.[26] 'Consistent with' and 'eventual' – this was looking down a long, foggy road. Mrs Thatcher and the MBC lobby had been repulsed. The attempt to 'control' sterling M3, the indicator of 'the money supply' chosen by the Treasury and the Bank of England, using high interest rates alone, would continue to be the government's policy. Recession and unemployment would reduce inflation.

NO PAIN, NO GAIN.

By the summer of 1980 it had become clear to the Thatcherites that sterling M3 was not behaving as their theories said it should. But it was not that Thatcher and Howe had lost touch with the real economic world. Mrs Thatcher tells us:

'On Wednesday, September 3 [1980] Geoffrey Howe and I met to discuss the monetary position... the money supply figures had

[22] Thatcher, Downing Street Years pp. 133 and 4.

[23] Philip Stephens p. 20

[24] David Smith p. 94

[25] Ibid.

[26] Ibid.

been rising much faster than the target we had set in the Medium Term Financial Strategy at the time of the March budget. It was hard to know how much of this was the result of our removing exchange controls in 1979 and our decision in June to remove the "corset" – a device by which the Bank of England imposed limits on bank lending.'[27]

She was right on both counts. Notice, too, that she said, 'Hard to know how much', not 'We wondered if any'. She had taken for granted that some of the problem was caused by removing exchange controls and abolishing the 'corset'. The techniques which would have controlled sterling M3, unfortunately, went completely against the grain of the ruling Tory group at the time. The ideologies of mainstream British political parties consist of a few over-arching concepts and buzz words which define the legitimate area of operations. For the Thatcherite Tories, freedom was the key concept, and the idea that removing exchange controls and removing the 'corset' – both acts increasing freedom, albeit the freedom of the banks – could be a bad thing was thus going to be hard to accept.

'Holidaying in Switzerland... Mrs Thatcher met Fritz Leutweilerm, head of the Swiss Central Bank, and the economist Professor Karl Brunner of Rochester University in the US... [who] both blamed the Bank of England, saying its method of controlling the money supply was all wrong. The answer to controlling inflation was to control the monetary base.'[28]

Thus fortified, Mrs Thatcher called a meeting in September 1980 to discuss MBC again. At that meeting, according to one of its participants, Christopher Johnson,

'After a memorable debate with academics and City economists on 29 September 1980... the Bank and Treasury officials joined in rejecting the plan [MBC] as impracticable, to Mrs Thatcher's disappointment.'[29]

Mrs Thatcher then faced the most awkward of choices. She knew their present policies, the policies of the London financial

---

[27] Thatcher, Path to Power p. 125

[28] Keegan 1985, p. 153. I rather doubt this 'holidaying' story. Mrs Thatcher hated holidays. More likely she was at the annual gathering of the Mount Pelerin Society, worshipping at the shrine of Hayek. On Pelerin see Cockett.

[29] Johnson p. 34.

sector, mediated through her Chancellor, were wrecking the domestic economy. On the other hand, she apparently could not persuade (or force) them to adopt her policy – some people you just cannot 'hand-bag' it seems – and thus had to make the best of a bad job. She looked for the get-out clause that would rationalise her defeat. She found hers in 'Monetary analysts [who] argued that both of these liberalisations had misleadingly bloated the sterling M3 figures.'[30]

Reality can be ignored: the figures are not real. The real, underlying sterling M3 was alright beneath this misleading, bloating effect.[31] She also fended off the idea of re-imposing the so-called 'corset' on bank lending with an extraordinarily feeble quip she made to Brain Walden: 'a corset is there to conceal the underlying bulges, not to deal with them, and when you take it off you might see that the bulges are worse'.[32] Economic policy by metaphor!

On 16 November 1980 the Bank of England finally reduced the Minimum Lending Rate from 14%. This, argues David Smith, was a direct consequence of the notorious speech calling for a 'bare knuckle fight' with the government over economic policy made by the Director General of the CBI, and the Chair of ICI warning Mrs Thatcher that the recession was so serious his company was about to announce a third quarter loss.[33] She had already admitted to leaders of the CBI that she was concerned about interest rates and the exchange rate.[34] This interest rate reduction is now seen as the end of the monetarist experiment, for the monetary figures did not justify the rate cut.

Eight days later, on 24 November 1980, Chancellor Howe announced a number of minor economic changes, framed by the explanation that 'These steps would be consistent with the gradual evolution towards a monetary base system and will help to judge how far such a system will contribute towards our medium-

---

[30] Thatcher, Downing Street Years p. 125

[31] This is as classic a case of psychological denial as you are ever likely to get. Mrs Thatcher represented the pre-Freudian, pre-war world. This was undoubtedly part of her appeal.

[32] Downing Street Years p. 125

[33] Smith p. 98

[34] Macdougal p. 248

term monetary objectives.'[35] This may have sounded like progress to Mrs Thatcher: at last her Chancellor was actually talking about moving towards a monetary base system. But in his memoir Nigel Lawson drawls, 'An experienced Whitehall watcher would have seen that this was in fact the thumbs down for MBC.'[36]

Evidently not as experienced a Whitehall watcher as Lawson, the Prime Minister and her closest political allies tried again to impose MBC on the system – and hopefully reduce the interest rates which were still crippling the British domestic economy (but making a fortune for the banks). They commissioned Professor Jurg Niehans, a Swiss monetarist, recommended by Walters, John Hoskyns and Alfred Sherman of the Centre for Policy Studies, to study the British system and its experience since the Tories took office. In Mrs Thatcher's account of it, Niehans report had 'a clear message':

'... North Sea oil had probably not been a major factor in sterling's appreciation: rather, tight monetary policy [i.e. high interest rates] had caused the pound to rise so high, imposing such pressure on British industry and deepening the recession. The report argued that we should use the monetary base rather than sterling M3 as the main monetary measure and suggested that we should allow it to rise in the first half of 1981. In short, Professor Niehams thought monetary policy was too tight and should quickly be loosened. Alan [Walters] emphatically agreed with him.'[37]

Notice that she cannot bring herself to write 'high interest rates' – which is the actual cause – and uses the euphemism 'tight monetary policy'. Yet Niehans came and went and nothing changed.[38] Lawson signals the importance of this episode by omitting it entirely from his memoir.[39] In late 1981 there were rumours

[35] Lawson p. 85

[36] Ibid.

[37] Thatcher, Downing Street Years, pp. 133 and 4. In June that year Niehans repeated at the LSE the seminar he had given in private in February. See the Guardian, June 27 1981. On the Niehans report see also Keegan 1985 p. 160.

[38] The Economics Editor of the Sunday Times commented on 14 June 1981, that 'There will be no further step towards monetary base control...'

[39] Mrs Thatcher and Walters tried once again, in 1985, to get MBC off the ground, but, says Lawson, 'The issue was satisfactorily put to bed with the promise of "further studies" of the US and German systems.' Lawson p. 480, emphasis added.

- presumably from the Thatcher camp – that Thatcher ally and MBC advocate Gordon Pepper would be the next Governor of the Bank of England.[40] But Mrs Thatcher failed to get her way on that one, too. By then she had been defeated. The first big interest group Mrs Thatcher took on was the City-Treasury-Bank of England-nexus – and she was defeated. She learned her lesson and never went up against them again until the battle over the European Monetary System.

I do not know whether MBC alone would have worked. What is interesting about the struggle is the way the financial system worked to prevent a return to the kind of physical controls it had succeeding in getting rid of in 1971 and 1979/80.

COCK-UP OR CONSPIRACY OR ...?

So what had really happened between 1979 and 1981? The conventional view is that the Tory economics team made a mistake. William Keegan can speak for this view.

'What the Medium Term Financial Strategy had failed to take account of was the crucial importance of the exchange rate... because the figures [in 1979-81] for the growth of money supply were running well above the targets in Lawson's MTFS, interest rates were kept high, attracting overseas funds to London, and maintaining the pound at a level where it continued to cause serious damage to industry. Monetary policy was in fact tight, but not according to the MFTS.'[41]

This is tacitly conceded by Thatcher:

'Before the end of Geoffrey Howe's Chancellorship the value of the pound against other currencies – the exchange rate – was also being taken into account.'[42]

Astonishingly, for some – by inference, most – of the Chancellor of the Exchequer's first term of office, the exchange rate was not only not being given economic priority, it was not even being taken into account. This is a unique, indeed bizarre

---

40 See, for example, the half page devoted to his views in Guardian, 6 November, 1981, where he is described as 'a potential governor of the Bank of England'. I don't know why he was not appointed. Mrs Thatcher does not mention this in her memoirs.

41 Keegan 1989, p. 71.

42 Thatcher, Downing Street Years, pp. 688 and 9.

event for a country which trades as much of its Gross Domestic Product as Britain. David Smith:

'Given Britain's post-war history of currency pressures, it was incredible that it took several years and two Conservative Chancellors before it was admitted that the pound was, after all, more important than domestic monetary targets.'[43]

But Smith has missed the point. Howe and Lawson had no target figure for the exchange rate so long as sterling rose. As Lawson makes clear in his memoir, they welcomed a rising pound. But as they showed in October 1981 when the pound began to fall, suddenly they did have a target figure, and interest rates went back up from 14% to 16%. The reduction granted the previous year at the climax of the complaints about the damage to British industry was immediately cancelled when the value of the pound was threatened. Looking back on the Thatcher/Lawson decade in The Times in 1993, Anatole Kaletsky presented two illustrations, one showing the behaviour of sterling, the other the behaviour of interest rates. They were headed, 'A decade of monetary mismanagement. Whenever the pound fell towards competitive levels... interest rates needlessly shot up.'[44]

There was no mistake. Mrs Thatcher, reluctantly, ended up fronting for the City's reassertion of its power – just as Mr Heath had done. Only Mrs Thatcher was unable to change course, not least because had she done so she would have been compared to the despised Mr Heath; and unlike him she had the revenues of North Sea oil with which to pay the unemployment benefit for the victims of her Treasury Ministers' policies towards the domestic economy.

---

[43] Smith p. 154.

[44] The Times 21 October 1993/40 See, for example, the half page devoted to his views in Guardian, 6 November, 1981, where he is described as 'a potential governor of the Bank of England'. I don't know why he was not appointed. Mrs Thatcher does not mention this in her memoirs.

Chapter Six

CIA AND MI5

At the end of the 1970s the Labour Left believed the Wilson-Callaghan Governments had betrayed the party and socialism with a series of sell-outs in the 1960s and 1970s, exemplified by the introduction of public spending cuts imposed by the International Monetary Fund (IMF) in 1976.[1] The Labour betrayal myth was a major factor in the party's turn inwards. The factionalised Labour Party of the late 1970s and early 1980s failed to show the electorate that the mess of the 1974-79 period was overwhelmingly the result of Conservative not Labour policies.

The Heath inflation was buried under the images of 'the Winter of Discontent'. It is still not understood by the bulk of the Labour Party, let alone the electorate, that the Callaghan-Wilson Government of the 1970s had, more or less, done what they set out to do – slowly bring down Heath's inflation without wrecking the economy.[2] In the House of Commons on 25 June 1996, David Evans, a Tory MP, stood up and asked Prime Minister John Major, 'Was it a Tory government under which inflation reached 26%?'.

---

[1] With pleasing symmetry the Tory Right believed Edward Heath betrayed Toryism with his so-called U-turn, the attempt at an incomes policy, his Industry Bill, the explosion of inflation and so forth. In a recent retrospective on the Heath years, Sir Geoffrey Howe spoke of 'the sense of betrayal which was felt by people like Nicholas Ridley, and Jock Bruce-Gardyne and Ian Gow.' All three were important members of the original Thatcher group. See Kandiah (ed.) pp. 191 and 2. In the same symposium the journalist Hugo Young said that 'the dynamism of Thatcherism related to what is adherents perceived to be the betrayal of what had happened at Selsdon Park.'

[2] What would happen when it is tried quickly was tested to destruction by Thatcher, Howe and Lawson.

The Conservative MPs shouted, 'No'. From the Labour benches there was silence. The inflation may have reached its peak under the Labour Government but it was caused by its predecessor. It seems that this elementary and central fact of recent political history is still not understood by the Parliamentary Labour Party.

Fuelled by the betrayal myth, the Labour Left pushed the party left-wards up to the disastrous general defeat of 1983. Becoming anti-EEC (once again) and pro-unilateral disarmament (one again), it was rejecting two of the central planks of the Atlantic alliance – and the central planks of the US-supported social democrat wing of the Parliamentary Labour Party.

More importantly, it was adopting two of the policies which the London media regarded – and still regard – as 'extreme'. These two policy changes in particular convinced the so-called Gang of Four, Roy Jenkins, William Rogers, Shirley Williams and David Owen to leave the Labour Party and form the Social Democratic Party (SDP) in 1981 – ensuring Labour's defeat at the 1983 General Election; but from their point of view, also maintaining Britain's role as an EEC member and reliable ally of the USA.[3]

The formation of the SDP had been a long time a-coming. It can be traced back through its personnel to the Gaitskellites of the 1960s who had never really accepted that they lost control of the party after Gaitskell's death, and back from there into the US post-war operations in Britain.

IMPOSING US HEGEMONY

In the post-war period the US government made a remarkable and very largely successful attempt to impose its ideology – and its capital – on the people of the non-communist world and especially Western Europe.

Undamaged by the war, in 1945 the US was producing something like half the world's GDP. In so doing it had created a booming domestic economy and sections of its elite's planners spent the war years working out how to ensure that this boom

---

[3] The significance of the nuclear issue is generally ignored in the accounts of this event. For an important corrective view, re-establishing the importance of the nuclear issue in the formation of the SDP, see Tom Easton's 'Who were they travelling with?' in Lobster 31.

continued.[4] They concluded that this could only be achieved by getting the rest of the world to continue consuming US goods at war-time levels of production. In the immediate post-war years they were the piper and they tried to call the tune, creating a large propaganda and intelligence operation in Western Europe which accompanied dollar loans and American goods into the war-ravaged European economies.[5]

One feature of this was the Labour Attaché programme which was established towards the end of the war. In the words of one its creators, Philip Kaiser, 'the labor attaché is expected to develop contacts with key leaders in the trade union movement, and to influence their thinking and decisions in directions compatible with American goals...'[6] The first US Labour Attaché in London was Sam Berger, who, in the words of Denis Healey, 'exerted an enduring influence on British foreign policy.'[7] Philip Kaiser commented that Berger 'had extraordinary access to many members of the [Attlee] cabinet, including the prime minister. It was universally recognised that he was the key member of our embassy.'[8] There were also Labour Information Officers attached to the Marshall Plan staff in the US Embassy in London promoting social democrats within the British Labour movement.[9]

The US post-war penetration of the British Labour Party and wider trade union movement climaxed with Joe Godson, who was Labour Attaché in London from 1953-59. Godson became very close to the Labour Party leader Hugh Gaitskell – to the point where Gaitskell and Godson were writing Labour Party policies

---

[4] See Shoup and Minter. Full employment meant not only profitability, it meant that the rumblings of social discontent of the depression years would remain muted. Although this is rarely discussed in mainstream US history books, the US came much closer to serious social upheaval - revolution would be an exaggeration - in the depression than did the UK.

[5] The best account of this is in Carew.

[6] Kaiser p. 113 'The labor attaché... had.. .an unusual opportunity to enhance American influence among individuals and institutions that historically have no contact with US diplomatic missions'. Ibid. p. 119

[7] Denis Healey p. 113. Berger has two innocuous entries in the Gaitskell Diaries, and the footnote from the editor, Philip Williams, on p. 120 that he was 'first secretary at the US Embassy', concealing his true role.

[8] Kaiser p. 120

[9] Carew pp. 128 and 9

and planning campaigns against their enemy, Labour left-winger Aneuran Bevan.[10] It may even be more complex than this for there is evidence that the Labour Attaché posts have been used as cover by the CIA.[11] It was about the CIA – but not just them. The CIA was only one of many agencies working in Britain in the post-war years. Labour Attachés reported, formally anyway, to the State Department. In the end, would it make any difference to know that Joe Godson had really been a genuine employee of the State Department, and not CIA under cover as we might have once suspected?

Large numbers of Labour MPs and trade unionists were paid to visit the United States. Among the Gaitskellite grouping in the Parliamentary party, Gaitskell, George Brown, Anthony Crosland and Douglas Jay all made visits.[12] Under the umbrella of just one minor aspect of the Marshall Plan, the Anglo-American Council on Productivity, 900 people from Britain – managers and union officials – went on trips to the United States;[13] hundreds of trade unions officers visited the US in the fifties under the auspices of the European Productivity Agency; and groups of British union

---

[10] See Williams (ed.) The Diaries of Hugh Gaitskell. Godson's obituary is in The Times, 6 September 1986. Godson's son, Roy, who appears on the same trade union/spook circuit in the 1970s, married Sam Watson's daughter. Watson was one of the most important trade union leaders in the post-war period, Gaitskell's ally, chairman of the National Executive Committee's International Committee and a 'liaison officer' between the Parliamentary Labour Party and the major unions.

[11] Jonathan Kwitney of the Wall Street Journal tracked down one Paul Sakwa, the case officer for Irving Brown, the most important CIA agent in the labour movement in Europe. From being Brown's case officer in Washington, Sakwa went on to a post under cover as the Assistant Labour Attaché at the US Embassy in Brussels. Kwitney pp. 334 and 5

[12] There is no detailed examination of this as far as I know and I don't know how many such programmes were run. Roy Hattersley commented that his first visit to the US was paid for by 'something which was laughingly called The Young Leaders' Program'. The Guardian, 27 February 1995. In his memoir, A Bag of Boiled Sweets (Faber and Faber, 1995) pp. 77-8, the Conservative MP, Julian Critchley describes how, upon letting the Tory Party Whips know that he had never been to the United States, he was immediately fixed up with a six week freebie by the US Embassy in London.

[13] Carew p. 137

leaders were sent on a three month trade union programme run by the Harvard Business School.[14]

CIA BEGINS FUNDING THE NON-COMMUNIST LEFT

There was a European-wide – and world-wide – programme to boost the social democratic wings of socialist parties and movements:

'At Thomas Braden's suggestion and with the support of Allen Dulles and Frank Wisner, the CIA began its covert support of the non-Communist political left around the world – trade unions, political parties and international organisations of students and journalists.'[15]

The biggest of these programmes that we are aware of was the Congress for Cultural Freedom (CCF from here on) which promoted the British social democrats. The CCF organised large conferences all over the world and began publishing journals – in Britain, Encounter, which first appeared in 1953. Encounter became a major outlet for the 'revisionist' – i.e. anti-socialist, anti-nationalist, pro-American – thinking of the younger intellectuals around Labour leader Hugh Gaitskell, such as Peter Jay, Patrick Gordon-Walker, Roy Jenkins and Anthony Crosland, all of whom were in Harold Wilson's first cabinet in 1964.[16] Anthony Crosland was a member of the International Council of the CCF: his role, said the CIA officer who was running CCF, was 'encouraging

[14] Ibid. pp. 189 and 90. The British trade union whose leadership responded most enthusiastically to these American overtures was the General and Municipal Workers' Union (GMWU), now the GMB, and it 'provided from among its leading officials half the British participants in the university trade union courses at Harvard and Columbia...' Ibid. p. 191. GMWU General Secretary, Tom Williamson, was one of the participants at the first meeting of the Bilderberg Group in 1954. (Eringer p. 49) Other early British participants included Hugh Gaitskell and Dennis Healey, who discusses the Bilderberg meetings in his memoir, The Time of My Life.

[15] Smith, OSS p. 368.

[16] The 1955 CCF conference in Milan, 'The Future of Freedom', was attended by Crosland, Richard Crossman, Denis Healey, Roy Jenkins and W. Arthur Lewis MP. Labour Party leader Hugh Gaitskell attended the conferences in in 1955, '57, '58 and '62. Gaitskell, Jenkins, Crosland, Rita Hinden, Patrick Gordon-Walker, John Strachey, Dennis Healey and Roderick Macfarquhar were published in Encounter. See Coleman pp. 73, 100, 185.

sympathetic people' to attend CCF conferences.[17]

As well as Encounter there was the monthly Socialist Commentary as a vehicle for the anti-socialists in the Labour Party. William Gausmann, Labour Information Officer in the US London mission, was a member of the journal's editorial board.[18] The dominant figure in Socialist Commentary was its editor for 20 years, Rita Hinden, who had been co-founder of the Fabian Colonial Bureau in 1940. Hinden was also a participant in CCF functions, wrote for Encounter, and was described by the CIA officer in charge of CCF, Michael Josselson, as 'a good friend of ours', on whose advice the CIA 'relied heavily... for our African operations.'[19] On her death Denis Healey, who had written widely for Socialist Commentary's American counterpart, New Leader, said that 'Only Sol Levitas of the American New Leader had a comparable capacity for exercising a wide political influence with negligible material resources.' But as Richard Fletcher commented, 'He [Healey] obviously hadn't paid a visit to Companies House whose register shows that in recent years Socialist Commentary has been drawing on a capital reserve of over £75,000.'[20] (Healey was apparently also unaware that Sol Levitas was also funded by the CIA.)

By the mid-1950s there was a thriving social democratic network operating in and around the Labour Party in Britain and reaching out into the British and American states, both overt and covert, which were supporting it. The career of Saul Rose in this period illustrates this. After war-time service in Army Intelligence, Rose was a lecturer at Aberdeen University, before becoming the Labour Party's International Secretary for three years. He then moved to the then recently established St Anthony's College at

[17] Hirsch and Fletcher pp. 59 and 60

[18] Carew p. 245

[19] She visited India and Japan on a CCF-sponsored trip after the Suez crisis. Richard Fletcher in Agee (ed.), Dirty Work p. 195

[20] Hirsch and Fletcher p. 67. The accounts of Socialist Commentary were prepared by the accountancy practice of John Diamond MP, one of the leading Gaitskellites, who later joined the SDP and is now in the House of Lords. He was also, for example, the Honorary Treasurer of the Labour Committee for Europe. See Finer, Appendix 2. In this latter role John Campbell in his biography of Roy Jenkins, p. 51, states that Diamond was 'charged with raising money that did not come from the City of London.'

Oxford, one of two British institutions which sponsored Congress of Cultural Freedom seminars in the UK. The other was Ditchley Manor, Oxford. Both were outposts of the Foreign Office/MI6 network.[21] (Former MP Dick Taverne, mentioned recently that as as young man he went to a Young Fabian conference at the other major Foreign Office country retreat, Wilton Park...[22])

It is easy at this distance to be indignant about Labour politicians hob-nobbing with the CIA. But in 1955, say, when Saul Rose left his job as Labour's International Secretary, the media simply did not discuss the Anglo-American intelligence and security services. There were Americans with money scattered about the higher reaches of the Labour movement in Britain; but Americans with money had been in Britain since the war years. This was during the Cold War and some of them, the labour officers in one guise or another, were originally from the US labour movement. I think it likely that in the 1950s the Labour revisionists, the Hindens and Croslands, believed they were taking part in a 'liberal conspiracy' (the title of Coleman's study of CCF) against the Soviet Union, with progressive, democratic forces – people they perceived to be like themselves.

But from the CIA's point of view, they were being run in a covert operation. While this may have had as one of its aims the struggle against Stalinism, the Americans sponsored and funded the European social democrats not because they were social democrats, but because social democracy was the best vehicle for the major aim of the programme: to ensure that the governments of Europe continued to allow American capital into their economies with the minimum of restrictions. This aim the revisionists in the Labour Party chose not to look at. (This, perhaps, is a tribute to the skill of the US personnel running the operations.)

Looking at the networking of the social democrats in the these

---

[21] Coleman p. 260 for the CCF connection. St Anthony's, Richard Deacon wrote in his The British Connection, was 'an unofficial annexe of MI6 in the fifties.' p. 259.

[22] Dick Taverne, Institute for Historical Research (IHR) Witness Statement on CDS, 1990,

p. 8. On the history of Wilton Park see Dexter M. Keezer, A Unique Contribution to International Relations: the Story of Wilton Park, (McGraw-Hill, Maidenhead, Berkshire, 1973)

post-war years, the intimacy between US Labour Attaché, Joe Godson, and Labour leader Hugh Gaitskell, was just business as usual.

TAKING THE TEETH OUT OF BRITISH ECONOMIC NATIONALISM

The strategic significance for the United States of the British social democrats' version of socialism was its central conclusion that ownership of economic assets was no longer of paramount importance. (In the USA, sociologist Daniel Bell was arguing the same thesis, sponsored by the same people, under the rubric of 'the end of ideology' – a term which has begun to find its way into Tony Blair's speeches.) This was the key line for US capital which wanted to penetrate the world's markets and was meeting resistance from people who called them imperialists. To US capital, socialism was simply a form of anti-American, economic nationalism: communism a more extreme version of the same thing.[23] The US government only had one operating criterion where a foreign government was concerned: is it willing to give US capital a free hand or not?[24] As the history of US imperialism since the war shows, the US is uninterested in the ideology of host governments, and has supported everything from social democrats to the most feral, military dictatorships in South and Central America and Africa. These US operations in and around the British social democrats and in the union movement was 'Taking the teeth out of British socialism', as Richard Fletcher put it in 1977;[25] but it could just as accurately have been called 'Taking the teeth out of British economic nationalism'.

CDS BEGINS TO TAKE SHAPE

The US-supported drive by the revisionists in the Labour Party had its first major set-back with the rise of CND, climaxing with the famous narrow majority in favour of unilateral nuclear disarmament at the party conference in 1960. Hugh Gaitskell's leadership of the party had largely been defined by the struggle

---

[23] The best exposition of this thesis is Block.

[24] This was vividly illustrated in the 1970s by the amount of US capital going into the Soviet bloc to take advantage of low wage rates and - ironically - the absence of functioning trade unions.

[25] Richard Fletcher, 'Who Were They Travelling with?' in Hirsch and Fletcher.

with the Left (real and imaginary). He believed the Communist Party of Great Britain had infiltrated the Labour Party, and was manipulating the Labour Left gathered round the newspaper Tribune.[26] Therefore, to the Gaitskellites in the Labour Party the rise of CND was little more than another communist conspiracy.[27] In reponse to the rise of CND the Gaitskellites' formed a party faction, the Campaign for Democratic Socialism (CDS). What became the CDS began in February 1960 when William Rodgers, Secretary of the Fabian Society, a key part of the social democratic network in the UK, organised a letter of support for Gaitskell from prospective parliamentary candidates. They included:

- Maurice Foley, who had been Secretary of the British section of the European Youth Campaign from 1951-59,[28] and later became a Foreign Office Minister and trustee of the Ariel Foundation;[29]
- Bryan Magee, who subsequently became a Labour MP and then joined the SDP;
- Dick Taverne, who later stood against the Labour Party as Democratic Labour and joined the SDP;
- Shirley Williams, one of the 'Gang of Four', who founded the SDP.

On 24 November 1960, after the narrow defeat for Gaitskell's line at the conference, this group announced itself as the Campaign for Democratic Socialism (CDS), with Rodgers as chair.[30]

Ever since the Richard Fletcher article on CDS et al in 1977, there have been questions about how this operation was funded. In mid November 1960 – i.e. a fortnight after the launch – Rodgers 'reported to the steering committee that many small donations had been received, together with a large sum from a source who wished to remain anonymous' – apparently the hotelier Charles

---

[26] For this latter belief, to my knowledge, the Gaitskellites produced no evidence.

[27] Some of the Labour Right proved incredibly gullible when it came to this 'communist conspiracy', accepting as genuine the most obvious forgeries. See for example pp. 224-6 of Jack and Bessie Braddock's memoir The Braddocks, (Macdonald, London, 1963) for a particularly choice example, passed to them by J. Bernard Hutton, who fronted several such forgeries. Who produced the forgeries? We do not know, but my guess would be IRD.

[28] This was funded by the CIA, though Foley has denied knowing this. See Bloch and Fitzgerald p. 106

[29] On Ariel see ibid. pp. 151-2 and Kisch pp. 67-8.

[30] Haseler, Gaitskellites p. 211

Forte.[31]

This donation, whatever it was, enabled CDS to have 'field workers in the constituencies and unions, whom it supported with travelling expenses, literature and organisational back-up, and other publications, plus a regular bulletin campaign, circulated free of charge to a large mailing list within the movement. And all this was produced without a single subscription-paying member.'[32] John Diamond was the CDS fund-raiser.[33]

A 1961 letter in CDS Campaign announced support from 45 MPs, including Austen Albu (who wrote for IRIS, on which see below), Crosland, Diamond (who joined the SDP), Desmond Donnelly, who resigned in 1968; Roy Jenkins (founder and leader of the SDP), Christopher Mayhew (who joined the Liberals, later SDP) and Reg Prentice (who joined the Tories).[34]

The following year were added new MPs William Rodgers (another of the 'Gang of Four') and Dick Taverne (who defected as a Democratic Labour MP, later SDP) The Gaitskellites' historian, Stephen Haseler noted, 'The whole central leadership of the Party in Parliament, with the single exception of Wilson, were Campaign sympathisers.'[35] The CDS also had the support of at least half of the Labour Party's regional organisers, though how precisely many is in dispute.[36]

SPOOKS IN THE UNIONS

Working in some of the unions were clandestine anti-communist groupings, the best known of which were the Amalgamated Engineering Union (AEU)'s 'club',[37] and Industrial Research and Information Services (IRIS), the industrial wing of the anti-commu-

---

[31] Hirsch and Fletcher p. 62. See Forte p. 81 where Gaitskell writes, 'things have gone remarkably well inside the Party. And for this a very large amount of credit must go to our friends in the Campaign for Democratic Socialism, which you have helped so generously.' This is undated unfortunately, but from the context it is 1961 or thereabouts. Conspiracy theorists may wish to take the obvious step beyond the evidence: Forte fronted the money for the CIA.

[32] Hirsch and Fletcher p. 62

[33] Windlesham p. 107. See also note 20 above.

[34] Haseler, Gaitskellites, p. 217

[35] Ibid. p. 219

[36] Shaw fn 150, p. 331

[37] On which see Wigham p. 128 and Minkin p. 180.

nist group Common Cause.[38] Charles Pannell, Secretary of the Parliamentary Trade Union Group of MPs and an Amalgamated Engineering Union (AEU)-sponsored MP, told the American academic Irving Richter, of his 'close relationship' with the General Secretary of the AEU, Cecil Hallett,[39] and of their combined efforts to defeat the left in the industrial and political wings of the movement, by building IRIS 'cells'. Pannell claimed that he, Hallett, and the IRIS cells working inside the AEU, were crucial in overturning the AEU's 1960 vote for CND, so restoring the Labour Party's policy to being pro-nuclear and pro-NATO. [40]

Though the clandestine involvement of the CIA is rarely visible, Hallett described a meeting between IRIS and the Trade Union Group of MPs in 1955 addressed by the CIA's labour man in Europe, Irving Brown.[41] After the 1960 Party conference 20 members of the TUC General Council signed a statement supporting NATO. Four of them, James Crawford, Harry Douglass, John Boyd and Sid Greene, were or were to become, officers of IRIS: a fifth, Sir Tom O'Brien, was still on the notepaper of Common Cause.

The only account from a participant in these union operations we have is from Peter E. Newell. In the 1950s Newell was an active member of the anti-Stalinist, Socialist Party of Great Britain. He worked as a draughtsman but wanted a change of career. It was suggested to him that he join the Post Office. Initially not keen on what he saw as a downward move, he has recalled how:

'quite subtly (I now realise) it was suggested that once in the PO, I would soon be able to write for The Post, the official fortnightly journal of the UPW [Union of Post Office Workers] – and be paid for it!'[42]

He duly joined the Post Office, was contacted by Norman Stagg, the editor of the journal, almost immediately, and began writing an anonymous, anti-communist column for it under the

---

[38] I believe that Common Cause was a CIA operation in the UK but the evidence supporting this view, though quite substantial, is circumstantial. For what there is see my Clandestine Caucus pp. 7-10.

[39] Hallett was on the Common Cause council in the fifties.

[40] Richter pp. 144 and 5

[41] Ibid. p. 41

[42] Letter to the author.

by-line of 'Bellman'. Stagg provided source material from the ICFTU, IRIS and the AFL-CIO. At the time the Union of Post Office Workers was a member of the trade union international body Postal, Telegraph and Telephone International. (PTTI) Like many of the these international trade union organisations, the PTTI was penetrated – or run – by the CIA.[43] Its president was the late Joe Beirne of the Communication Workers of America. Beirne was also founder and Secretary-Treasurer of American Institute for Free Labor Development (AIFLD), created and run by the CIA. As far as it is possible to be sure of anything in this field without a confession from the man himself or his case officer, Joe Beirne was a major asset of the CIA in the American and world labour movements.[44]

CLIMAX – AND ANTI-CLIMAX

What Eric Shaw calls social democratic centralism, the attempt by the social democratic right to police the entire Labour Party and trade union membership, peaked in 1962. In March 1961 five MPs, including future party leader Michael Foot, were expelled from the Parliamentary Party for voting against the Tory Government's defence estimates. The Gaitskellites repulsed the unilateralists at the annual conference that year; and in the Labour Party its 'personnel committee', the Organisational Sub-committee, was dominated by Ray Gunter MP[45] and George Brown, a 'CIA source',[46] and serviced by the Party's National Agent's Department, which received information from the Foreign Office/MI6 psy-war outfit, the Information Research Department (IRD), and Special Branches, among others.[47] Determined upon a final purge of the Parliamentary Party, George Brown approached MI5, via the journalist Chapman Pincher, for evidence of Soviet

[43] See Agee, CIA Diary p. 618.

[44] On the late Joseph Beirne and CIA see Counterspy, February 1974 pp. 42 and 43 and May 1979 p. 13, and Agee CIA Dairy, p. 603. On AIFLD see Fred Hirsch 'The Labour Movement: Penetration Point for US Intelligence and Transnationals' in Hirsch and Fletcher, and 'The AFL-CIA' by former US Air Force Intelligence officer Winslow Peck in Frazier (ed.) Newell was introduced to Beirne at the UPW conference at Blackpool.

[45] In 1968 he became a director of IRIS.

[46] Bower, p. 356

[47] Shaw pp. 58 and 9.

links to Labour MPs believed to be 'fellow travellers'. But MI5 declined to provide it, apparently afraid that to do so would reveal their sources within the PLP. With the Macmillan Government in what appeared to be terminal decline, Gaitskell died suddenly and the right in the Parliamentary Party – and the Anglo-American intelligence and security services – saw the party leadership slip from the Gaitskellites' hands as Harold Wilson won the leadership election and then the general election of 1964.

The social democratic wing of the Labour Party had two key positions: British membership of NATO and retention of British nuclear weapons; and membership of the EEC. After the defeat of CND at the Labour conference of 1961 it was European Economic Community (EEC) membership which became their great cause. Support for EEC membership within the Labour Party had been formally organised first in 1959 by the Labour Common Market Committee (founders Roy Jenkins, Jack Diamond and Norman Hart), which became the Labour Committee for Europe in the mid-1960s.[48] European unity had been one of the projects favoured by the USA, looking for good anti-Soviet alliances in the early post-war era, and the European Movement had been funded by the CIA.[49] As well as receiving the support of the US, in the 1960s Gaitskellites Roy Jenkins, Shirley Williams and William Rodgers were among the regular attendees of the annual Anglo-German Konigswinter conferences.[50] This time the social democrats were being supported by the British Foreign Office, which had decided by then that, whether they liked it or not – and they didn't – their future lay in the Common Market.

The CDS, the Gaitskellites, never accepted Wilson as the legitimate leader of the Labour Party and plotted constantly against him. The personnel of the Gaitskellites, the Labour Committee on Europe and the CDS were virtually identical.[51] In the 1960s Harold Wilson identified as the group working against him as CDS.[52] When

[48] See note 20 above. Diamond was also the fund raiser for CDS.

[49] See 'The CIA backs the Common Market' in Agee (ed.) Dirty Work, pp. 201-3 and Hirsch and Fletcher.

[50] Bradley p. 52

[51] With a number of important qualifications. Hugh Gaitskell, for example, was not pro-EEC membership.

[52] Dorril and Ramsay p. 188

the group formally broke up it continued as a dining club, the 1963 Club. In the early 1970s Tony Benn identified them as 'the old Campaign for Democratic Socialism-Europe group'.[53]

In 1970 the election of the Heath Government meant that another serious effort to get Britain in the EEC would be made and the issue would divide the Labour Party then in opposition. In early 1971 Tony Benn's diary records him talking with Roy Jenkins of the Common Market issue splitting the Labour Party.[54] Ten months later, on 10 October, after a pro- and anti-EEC clash in the Shadow Cabinet, Benn commented on the emergence of 'a European Social Democrat wing in the Parliamentary Party led by Bill Rodgers.'[55] This group formally announced itself on 28 October when 69 pro-EEC Labour MPs voted with the Conservative Government in favour of entry into the EEC in principle. From then on the group operated as a party within a party, with William Rodgers acting as an unofficial whip.[56]

In 1971, 72 and 73 various members of the Gaitskellites approached Roy Jenkins to leave Labour and start a new party. On each occasion he declined to do so.[57] In 1973, however, helped by Sir Fred Hayday, former chair of the TUC, and Alf Allen, future chair of the TUC, Jenkins did 'set up an institutional framework' with 'moderate' trade union leaders – a regular dining group in the Charing Cross Hotel.[58]

In December 1974 the Manifesto Group was formed within the PLP. Described by Barbara Castle as 'a group of middle-of-the-road and right-wing Labour MPs [which] had been meeting to discuss how to counter the growing influence of the left-wing Tribune group of MPs', [59] its chair was Dr Dickson Mabon, who

[53] Ibid.

[54] Benn, Office Without Power p. 324 and 5

[55] Ibid. p. 381

[56] Bradley pp. 53-5. As early as 1970 some of that group had begun trying to get him to lead the formation of a new party. 'Dick Taverne recalls a meeting of pro-Marketeers in his flat to discuss tactics as early as June 1970.' Ibid. Jenkins in his memoir on 1973: 'Excluding the possibility of forming an independent party, which at that stage neither I nor my supporters were remotely prepared for...' p.360 (Emphasis added). Not that he found it unacceptable...

[57] Jenkins p. 354

[58] Bradley p. 53

[59] Bradley p. 53

joined the SDP; its Secretary was John Horam, who became a Tory Minister in 1995, and two of its most active members were CDS enthusiasts, bearers of the Gaitskellite torch, David Marquand and Brian Walden. [60]

In Jenkins' memoir there are some wistful remarks on '1975 as a great missed opportunity for Heath and Whitelaw and a whole regiment of discarded Conservative "wets" as much for Shirley Williams and Steel and me.'[61] Jenkins was looking back on the 1975 Common Market referendum campaign during which he found it more congenial working with pro-EEC Tories and Liberals than he did with the left-wing of his own party;[62] and there is a large hint in Thatcher's second volume of memoirs, that some kind of centrist realignment in British politics was attempted on the back of the referendum.[63] Mrs Thatcher knew that such talk was taking place because she was part of some of it. In December 1976 Jenkins' ally, Reg Prentice, was discussing how to bring down the Callaghan Government with, inter alia, Tory MPs Julian Amery and Maurice Macmillan, and Gaitskellite Labour MPs Walden and the late John McIntosh.[64] Stephen Haseler, whose information on this comes from Prentice's diaries, tells us:

'For some years past the arguments for a realignment had been taken seriously by a section of the Conservative Party who had been close to Macmillan.'[65]

Prentice proposed that Jenkins form a coalition with Margaret

---

[60] Jenkins p. 354. In the CDS 'witness seminar', p. 27, William Rodgers stated that CDS had a 'very close working relationship with Fred Hayday of the General and Municipal Workers'.

[61] Castle, Diaries p.156

[62] Bradley p. 60. With the exception of Giles Radice and George Robertson, both GMWU/GMB-sponsored, the whole of the active leadership of the Manifesto Group subsequently defected to the SDP. At time of writing, 1998, Robertson is Minister for Defence and Radice is Chairman of the European Movement in the UK.

[63] Jenkins pp. 425-6

[64] On 14 October 1975 Tony Benn records in his diary: 'Robert Kilroy-Silk, Labour MP for Ormskirk, told me that £2 million had been left unspent by the pro-Market lobby and it was a fund of which the trustees were Heath, Thorpe and Jenkins… the rumour was that if Wilson moved too far to the Left they would use the money to set up a new party.'

[65] See The Path to Power, p. 331.

Thatcher as leader and talked to her about this. But, on Prentice's account, haunted by memories of 1931 and the fate of Ramsay MacDonald, Jenkins declined again.

When Harold Wilson resigned in 1976, Jenkins stood for leader of the Labour Party, lost as he knew he would, and took the exit door opened for him by Harold Wilson – going to Brussels as President of the EEC. Jenkins bailed out at a good time, for the pro-Common Market wing of the Labour Party was losing the fight against the left in the Parliamentary Labour Party. In 1977 some of the Gaitskellite pro-Europe group of MPs formed the Campaign for a Labour Victory, 'in many ways a resurrection of the of the Campaign for Democratic Socialism'.[66] William Rodgers' PA was one of the chief organisers and it set up its office in the HQ of the EETPU.[67] Its full-time organiser was Alec McGivan who became the first full-time worker for the SDP, four years later. This was the SDP in embryo.

Around Jenkins in exile gathered some of the Gaitskellites. Mike Thomas, a Labour and then SDP MP:

'there in fact were a group of people working with Roy Jenkins outside parliament, most of whom were known to many of us, friends of ours, some who were less well-known, in the SDA or elsewhere'.[68]

The SDA was the Social Democratic Alliance, formed in 1975 by two London Labour Party members and local councillors; Stephen Haseler, who had written a history of the Gaitskellites, and Douglas Eden. They took up the struggle with the Labour Left on the ground. There has been no history of the SDA and the official historians of the SDP seem curiously reluctant to acknowledge its role. It attracted support from the union right[69] – and from other, more surprising sources, including Brian Crozier,

[66] Haseler, Battle for Britain, pp. 59 and 60. Amery was a former SIS officer and a friend of the former Deputy Chief of SIS, the late George Kennedy Young, who was then machinating against the Labour Government with his Unison Committee for Action. Maurice Macmillan had been a director of one of the IRD front companies and had also been involved in the attempt in the mid-1974 to launch a government of national unity to prevent the re-election of Harold Wilson.

[67] Ibid.

[68] Bradley p. 59

[69] 'How Frank Chapple says on top', New Statesman, 25 July 1980

MI6 and CIA asset, one of the leading figures in the psy-war campaign about the 'communist threat'.[70] Like Crozier, Haseler and Eden claimed to perceive a serious threat from the Labour Left. In 1976 Haseler wrote in The Times:

'we may now be on the verge of an economy which will remove itself from the Western trading system by import controls, strict control of capital movements and eventually non-convertibility of the currency. At home this will involve rationing, the direction of capital and labour and the final end of the free trade union movement.'[71]

'May be on the verge of' something is neither precise nor a great rallying cry for action, but the SDA was very definitely 'on message' as far as the media was concerned and got much publicity for their part in the great hunt for the subversive menace within the Labour Party then being mounted by the likes of Brian Crozier, MI5, bits of the CIA et al.[72]

In November 1979, after Jenkins' had been given the Dimbleby Lecture on BBC TV in which to more or less announce his intention of forming a social democratic party, businessman Clive Lindley and London Labour Councillor Jim Daley, both of whom had been active in the Campaign for Labour Victory, [73] set up the Radical Centre for Democratic Studies, 'a press cutting and information service on the political scene in Britain' and a support group for Jenkins.[74] Finally a group met to discuss forming the new party. From the Social Democratic Alliance there was Stephen Haseler; from Roy Jenkins' UK support group, Clive Lindley and Jim Daley; David Marquand, Jenkins' PA in Brussels, and Lord Harris, who had been Jenkins' PR man in the 1960s. This was the core of Jenkins' network plus Haseler.

Forming the SDP in 1981 probably ensured that Labour would lose the next general election. To make certain, members of the

[70] Crozier's memoir describes much of this.

[71] The Times 29 April 1976. See Crozier pp. 147-8. This account of Crozier's has not been faced by the historians of the period. Haseler left the UK after the formation of the SDP to spend a year at the US Heritage Foundation. Heritage looks like a CIA psy-war operation, and I have been told that it is, but no evidence exists.

[72] This period is described in detail in Dorril and Ramsay.

[73] Owen p. 457

[74] Bradley p. 73

Labour Right had taken other steps to ensure a Labour defeat. In 1980, after the decision had been by the Jenkins group taken to form a new party, there was a contest for the leadership of the Labour Party between Denis Healey of the centre-right coalition and Michael Foot of the centre-left coalition. Foot just won – by the votes cast for him by seven Labour MPs who subsequently defected to the Social Democratic Party. Neville Sandelson, one of the seven, who revealed this, said:

'Myself and my colleagues who voted for Foot were leaving the Labour Party and setting up a new party under the leadership of the Gang of Four and it was important that we finished off the job. It was very important that the Labour Party as it had become was destroyed.'[75]

Some of the Labour Right who had not defected to the SDP, who had just seen their candidate, Denis Healey, lose the leadership contest, then made sure the Labour Party had not only a left-wing leader, but also a left-wing manifesto for the 1983 General Election. At the 1983 meeting between the Shadow Cabinet and the National Executive Committee to finalise the manifesto for the forthcoming election, John Golding, from what Roy Hattersley called 'the hard right', proposed adopting all the policies being suggested by the Left. This was carried with virtually no discussion: the great left-right struggle over the manifesto which Roy Hattersley had been anticipating, did not materialise. The Right had decided that since they were going to lose the election anyway they would see that it was lost with all the Bennite Left's policies attached to it.[76] The 1983 Labour election manifesto, the so-called longest suicide note in history, was written by the Right, as well the Left.

In his review of the Ivor Crewe and Anthony King history of the SDP, Tom Easton lists the US connections to the key figures in the SDP's formation and comments:

'In this context... we can perhaps begin to see the rise of the SDP as a rather more strategic development than the 'fated to fail' warring personalities explanation of Crewe and King. It begins to

---

[75] The Sunday Telegraph 14 January 1996

[76] Roy Hattersley told this story in 'Comrades At War', part 2 of the series The Wilderness Years, BBC2, December 1995. He was told of the strategy by John Golding after the meeting.

to be possible to see where the many assorted [Joe] Godson outfits, the Haseler activities, the Trilateralists','crisis of democracy' outpourings and the much-hyped revulsion at Labour and Liberal [anti-nuclear] activities, begin to take some coherent shape.'[77]

The shape is familiar. For, from the 1950s and the struggles with the Bevanite left, the social democrats portrayed themselves as being engaged in a struggle with communism in Britain. For the US and UK states, 'communism' provided the means to attack the opponents of imperialism, not for their views but for their alleged support of a foreign/alien power and ideology. From the immediate post-war years through to Mrs Thatcher's description of the NUM as the 'enemy within' in 1984, the 'communist menace' was used by the British Right and the secret arms of the British state in its struggle against the Left.

If 1980/1 is remembered on the British Left for the explosion of CND membership, it also saw the beginning of a massive outflow of capital from the UK with the abolition of exchange controls, and renewed enthusiasm for the Special Relationship with the United States; enthusiasm expressed by a willingness to follow the US in increasing arms expenditures. Though not directly causally linked, they are parts of a wider, unified whole.

The revitalisation of the global military structure needed to police the American economic empire provoked a revival of opposition to it in much of Western Europe. In Britain (as elsewhere in Western Europe) this sent the state off again to smear the opposition – the so-called 'peace movement' – all over Europe as 'communist'. The left/'peace movement' opposition to nuclear weapons in the early 1980s was a serious challenge. It threatened not a Soviet invasion of Western Europe – hardly anybody in NATO actually believed there was the remotest chance of that – let alone a Soviet nuclear strike.

It was a threat to the support structure of the US economic empire; and in Britain, it was a threat to the role of the central power bloc most concerned with Britain's international role, the overseas lobby. To suggest Britain give up being a nuclear power, or shut-down the US bases, or withdraw from the US-dominated intelligence-gathering system is, ultimately, to suggest that the

[77] 'Who were they travelling with?' in Lobster 31.

British state concentrates on events within these shores and no longer provides the military, diplomatic, intelligence, legal, administrative and tax break support for the overseas sector of the economy. For the US, for NATO, and for the overseas lobby in Britain, opposing Britain's continued junior role in the Atlantic alliance was the same as not taking the 'Soviet threat' seriously enough, which was the same as being pro-communist.

The smear campaign against Harold Wilson began in earnest after he opposed the City and the Bank of England in the 1960s, refusing to make the cuts in public spending they sought. The 'communist threat' to Britain reached its hysterical peak in the mid-1970s as the Labour Party began to shift towards opposition to the central planks of the post-war international order. Among the many psy-war operations being run round that theme were the so-called 'private armies', all funded and run by City figures. The late David Stirling, who had tried to get GB75/Better Britain off the ground, received his funding from the City. The late G.K.Young who was running the Unison Committee for Action, had been a senior banker after leaving SIS as its Deputy Chief, and Unison's members included other City figures, including Anthony Cavendish; and much of General Sir Walter Walker's funding for his Civil Assistance came from the City.[78]

When the overseas lobby's interests were challenged by opposition to Britain's membership of the EEC, those opposing EEC membership were smeared as 'pro-communist', as two prominent members of the 'anti' campaign in the 1975 European referendum, Sean Stewart, in 1975 working for Labour Cabinet member Peter Shore, and Conservative MP Richard Body, discovered.[79] As Colin Wallace revealed in 1986/7, the 'communist smear' tactics were used by MI5 against a large cohort of Labour MPs – and some Liberals – in the 1970s.[80]

But to maintain the communist smear, to keep it potent, the 'Soviet threat' had to be perceived as real in some sense; and, equally important, there had to be a group in the UK supporting

[78] The details of this are in Dorril and Ramsay ch. 34

[79] Broad and Geiger (eds.) p. 59. This is peculiarly revealing for Peter Shore was the staunchest of Atlanticists, opposing the EEC in large part because of the damage he thought it would do to Britain's relationship with the USA!

[80] See Paul Foot's Who Framed Colin Wallace?

the Soviet Union with which individuals could be linked – an 'enemy within'. The Communist Party of Great Britain (CPGB) played this role, a role so important that MI5 helped sustain the CPGB as a significant force on the British Left.

In the midst of the Cold War, just after the Soviet suppression of the Hungarian uprising, MI5 learned of the existence of clandestine Soviet financial support for the Communist Party of Great Britain (CPGB). A man from the Soviet embassy delivered bags of used British notes to the CPGB. Peter Wright described this in Spycatcher in 1987, though its significance was missed at the time:

'Then there was the Falber affair. After the PARTY PIECE operation, MI5 went on the hunt for CPGB files which listed the secret payments made to the Party by the Soviets. We suspected that perhaps they might be held in the flat of Reuben Falber, who had recently been made cashier of the Russian funds.'[81]

MI5 knew about the payments, and knew Falber was in charge of them!

Wright's identification of Reuben Falber as the link with the Soviet embassy, was later confirmed by Falber himself, who also believes the state knew about the money. [82] All MI5 wanted were the accounts, the books – the evidence. Wright tells us that MI5 planned to burgle Falber's flat but their first plan failed – and leaves it there! To MI5 the proof of the Moscow Gold must have had something of the status of the Holy Grail; and we are to believe that having located it they made only one attempt to get it? Wright really wants us to believe that for 20 years, aware that the CPGB were getting actual Soviet cash money, MI5 made one failed attempt to get the records and just gave up? This is simply not credible.

Something similar happened in the United States. David J. Garrow described how the FBI recruited the brothers Jack and Morris Childs in the early 1950s.[83] The Childs had been in the

[81] Spycatcher p. 175

[82] Falber's account is in Changes, 16-19 November 1991. In it he writes: 'Did the authorities know about it [the Moscow money]? I think they did.'

[83] The FBI and Martin Luther King, Jr.: From "Solo" to Memphis,W.W. Norton, London and New York, 1981. Garrow estimated $1m a year were being supplied at one point, a figure confirmed later as an underestimate during the funding revelations at the end of the decade during the collapse of the Soviet Union.

CPUSA, Morris Childs rising to become editor of the US Daily Worker, but they had quit in 1947 after an internal dispute, and moved to the right. At the FBI's behest they rejoined the CPUSA in the early 1950s, quickly became significant figures again in the party, and ended up as the financial conduit between the Soviet government and the CPUSA: Morris Childs received the suitcases of dollars from the Soviets. Garrow comments:

'From [CPUSA head] Gus Hall Jack and Morris learned virtually everything that was occurring within the American Communist Party. Thus the FBI and the US executive branch knew the full story of the American party and witnessed first-hand the contacts of the domestic party with foreign powers... virtual control of the American CP... too valuable to be sacrificed for a public relations coup.' (p. 38)

There is no evidence that quite this level of control was exerted by MI5 on the CPGB. However, the large transmitter found attached to the bottom of the table in the CPGB's central meetings room, displayed by ex-CPGB Central Committee member George Matthews in The Independent (25 November 1989), illustrates Peter Wright's claim that, 'By 1955... the CPGB was thoroughly penetrated at almost every level by technical surveillance [i.e. bugs and taps] or informants'; and with the spreading disillusion in the 1950s, climaxed by Hungary, MI5 can have had no trouble recruiting active and former party members, like the late Harry Newton, to inform on the British comrades.[84]

There is no evidence that MI5 were running the CPGB. But it did allow the CPGB to run. For, had the existence of the 'Moscow gold' been revealed in 1958 or 9, coming after the Soviet invasion of Hungary, the CPGB would have been terminally damaged. But for MI5 the 'communist threat' – and the link to the Soviet Union - was simply too useful a stick with which to beat the much more important wider labour movement and Labour Party to be surrendered.

The Soviet connection with the CPGB enabled the Security Service to portray both the unions and the left of the Labour Party, a few of whom worked with the CPGB, as subversives; and with a subversive minority in its midst, this enabled the labour movement as a whole to be portrayed as a threat to the well-being

[84] Wright p. 175

of the nation.[85]

In effect the FBI and MI5 ran their respective Communist Parties as 'honey-traps' for the US and British Left. The American Communist Party does not seem to me to have been of much political importance. But while the precise extent of CPGB influence within the British labour movement is unclear,[86] it is indisputably the case that the CPGB did have influence on the left of the Labour Party – influence that certainly would have been much diminished and might not have occurred at all had the CPGB been revealed in the late 1950s as being secretly funded by the Soviet Union. Just as the Labour Party's transformation in 1983 into a party with a left manifesto and left leader would not have been accomplished without the help of some on the Party's Right, the CPGB's survival as a major force on the British Left was ensured by MI5 keeping the 'secret' of the CPGB's clandestine funding.

This episode raises in acute form the question of how much of what we take for granted as autonomous political activity in this country is being manipulated by the British and American secret states.

---

[85] This was a staple of the subversive-hunters in the mid 1970s. But compare and contrast Geoffrey Stewart-Smith's Not To Be Trusted: Left Wing Extremism in the Labour and Liberal Parties of February 1974, with his 1979 Hidden Face of the Labour Party. By 1979 he has added Trotskyist groups in the Labour Party to the CPGB as 'the threat'.

[86] I tried to assess this in Clandestine Caucus.

Chapter Seven

The Prawn Cocktail Offensive

After the 1983 election defeat, Labour's attitude to the European Economic Community was uncertain. The party and the Parliamentary Party – were divided. After the 1975 Referendum, the leadership had accepted the verdict of the electorate but by 1983 and the rise of the Bennite Left, the party had become 'anti' again. After the 1983 defeat a number of factors began to shift opinion in the Labour Party. The fact that the Labour Left's policies, including withdrawal from the EEC, had apparently been so heavily defeated in the election discredited their views. The party began to have success in European Parliamentary elections,[1] and small amounts of European money began to arrive in Britain, changing the attitude of Labour local authorities which were receiving nothing but cuts and criticism from London.

This shift was reflected inside the trade unions and by the end of 1984, while the TUC's General Congress remained against British membership, its full-time officials, the TUC Secretariat, were 'following a de facto pro-European policy.'[2] Under constant assault from the government, trade unions began to perceive that their future might be brighter in the EEC where they were seen to be legitimate, if minor, players. The financial deregulation of the 1980s and the explosion of financial speculation, facilitated by the computer chip, created a climate in which it became a commonplace to believe that the nation state, and thus national economic policies, were less and less viable.

[1] I remember how my local party's hostility to the EEC began to wane after election victory in the 1984 European Parliamentary election in Humberside.

[2] Teague p. 36

This line was skilfully used by the pro-Europe lobby to influence the growing 'green' awareness in the 1980s: arguments such as 'Pollution is a European problem and needs European solutions' became very common. All of this was massively reinforced when Mrs Thatcher began to be perceived as a 'little Englander', anti-Europe. Thatcher's support for the anti-EEC position contaminated it in the eyes of many in the party.[3] Finally, although it is not quite true that Labour under Neil Kinnock became pro-EEC because opinion polls showed the EEC to be popular, by the third election defeat in 1987, it is certainly the case that had opinion polls shown the EEC to be unpopular, Labour would not have supported membership. After the 1987 election defeat the Kinnock-led Parliamentary Party was not prepared to challenge public opinion in any major area.

The Wilson and Heath Governments had both tried to create a tri-partite alliance of domestic interests – unions, state and employers – to run the domestic economy, without seeking to confront the City-Bank of England-Foreign Office nexus, the overseas lobby. Labour's problem was that not only was it was too closely identified with the unions, a significant minority of its members and MPs were socialists and did not approve of working with capital, domestic or otherwise. Heath's difficulties lay in his party's identification with the financial and overseas apparatus in London which had little interest in the domestic manufacturing economy, and the significant minority of his party which did not approve of dealing with unions. Consequently, for both parties corporatism, as it became known, proved difficult to implement. Under Thatcher, the unions were declared 'the enemy within' and the financial/overseas sector was given everything it had always wanted: no exchange controls, high interest rates and no controls on lending with predictably – and predicted – disastrous consequences for the domestic manufacturing economy.

Underlying the British economic experience was the conflict between the interests of the overseas lobby, the City of London, and the domestic economy. This was understood by the Labour Left in the 1970s and expressed in the growth of the so-called Alternative Economic Strategy (AES) which was underpinned by

[3] Labour's shifting EEC policies are surveyed by Geddes. I discuss political 'contamination' below.

the the 'City versus Industry' argument, as it came to be known. By the mid-1980s Labour actually had come close to a radical, anti-finance capital, anti-overseas lobby, pro-domestic economic policy.[4]

There never was a single alternative strategy and calling it the AES is misleading. Most importantly this misses the distinction between Alternative Socialist Economic Strategies and the non-socialist variety. Both shared the hostility to the City/overseas lobby/finance and saw that sector's dominance as the problem, but they offered different solutions to it. Neil Kinnock, for example, was heavily influenced by the economist John Eatwell who, in the middle of the first Thatcher recession of the early 1980s, had written a book, Whatever Happened to Britain?,and produced a TV series with the same title. These argued that the recovery of the British economy centred on the reconstruction of manufacturing, and that this entailed the adoption of something like the German or French relationship between manufacturing and finance capital – views which were reflected in Neil Kinnock's 1986 book, Making Our Way.[5]

RISING STAR

In the Labour Party hierarchy, one of the rising stars was Bryan Gould, who, after being one of the successes of Labour's 1987 election campaign, topped the poll for election to the Shadow Cabinet that year. Gould was a 'moderniser'. After the 1987 election defeat, as part of the Policy Review, Neil Kinnock appointed Gould as chair of the central Policy Review committee, that dealing with the economy, industrial strategy and public ownership. This group included John Edmonds of the GMB union, Gordon Brown, now Chancellor of the Exchequer, and John Eatwell, who had become Neil Kinnock's personal advisor on economics, and who attended 'as an observer and as a link between the committee and Neil's office'.[6] Gould began work believing that the party leader and his personal advisor on economics agreed with his views. His team took the process seriously, commissioning 75

---

[4] See, for example, The City: A Socialist Approach, Report of the Labour Party Financial Institutions Study Group, published in 1982.

[5] Eatwell, Duckworth/BBC, 1982; Kinnock, Blackwell, Oxford, 1986

[6] Gould p. 205. Eatwell is now Lord Eatwell.

papers on the British economy, and produced a radical critique, emphasising the damage done to it by the dominance of the City – the views of chairman Gould.[7]

Unfortunately, this was not what the leadership then wanted to hear. Somewhere between writing their books and 1988, Kinnock and Eatwell had changed their minds, and concluded that if it could be achieved at all, the reconstruction of British manufacturing could only be achieved within the EEC.[8] Gould was aware of Kinnock's shifting view of membership of the EEC, but welcomed John Eatwell's presence at the group's activities because having read Eatwell's Whatever Happened to Britain?, he assumed that Eatwell thought like he did. But the massive amount of work done by the Gould group was for nought. The day before the document was due to go to the printer, Gould was asked to meet a 'Kinnock-inspired delegation'[9] of Eatwell, Gordon Brown and Tony Blair, who said that they felt the document should not go forward in its present form:

'They objected in particular to what remained of any commitment to return privatised industries to "some form of public ownership" and to the formula agreed for purchasing the 2% shareholding in British Telecom which would give a Labour Government a majority shareholding.'[10]

Gould rejected their approach – Blair was not even part of the committee which wrote the policy – but the document was watered down, and in the Autumn of 1988, a year after topping the poll for the Shadow Cabinet, Gould, who was both anti-EEC and anti-overseas lobby, was removed from his position on Labour's economics team, the first major casualty of the Labour leadership's embrace of EEC membership.

Shadow Chancellor John Smith had always been in the pro-EEC wing of the party, and after the 1987 general election defeat,

[7] The 75 figure is from Hughes and Wintour p. 131.

[8] Hughes and Wintour come close to implying that the shift to a pro-EEC position was taken because their polling of public opinion said it would be popular. See p. 184. Some reports date Neil Kinnock's move to a pro-European position as early as 1982. I am unable to date this change of mind precisely. Kinnock's foreword to his Making Our Way is dated September 1986; the démarche by Brown, Blair and Eatwell was around April 1988.

[9] Hughes and Wintour p. 132

[10] Gould p. 209

around Smith an Economic Secretariat had been created, made up of:

'full-time advisers with degrees in economics (sic)... supplemented by a network of high-powered economists, several of whom had previously believed that Britain should go it alone in a drive to expand the economy and reduce unemployment, but had now been won over to the stability and shelter of the European monetary system'.[11]

LABOUR PLUMPS FOR THE ERM

Smith was a very traditional Labour Party figure, an economics spokesperson who, knowing little about the subject, sought economic advice and fell into the hands of advisors from the City of London who are 'the experts'. By 1988 Kinnock and Smith (and their advisors) had concluded that Labour should become the party of Europe and Britain should join the European Exchange Rate Mechanism.[12] In 1971 Conservative MP Edward Du Cann was present when Conservative MPs were briefed on the meaning of the Competition and Credit Control proposals and saw that hardly anybody in the room had the faintest idea what was being discussed. Seventeen years later Bryan Gould had a similar experience:

'I remember [Gordon] Brown addressing the Parliamentary Labour Party on the great advantages of joining the ERM, using arguments I knew to be erroneous. He suggested that by fixing the parity within the ERM, we would be applying socialist planning to the economy, rather than leaving an important issue to market forces. The party responded warmly to the notion that speculators would be disarmed.

'They all seemed unaware that the only thing which gave speculators their chance was a government foolish enough to defend a parity seen to be out of line with a currency's real value... John Smith and Gordon Brown truly believed that the ERM was a new, magical device which would insulate their decisions about the

[11] McSmith p. 121 The fact that McSmith felt it worth mentioning that some of these advisers had degrees in economics speaks volumes about the general economic illiteracy taken for granted among the Parliamentary Labour Party.

[12] ERM policy was decided by 'Smith's team and John Eatwell who was working for Neil Kinnock.' McSmith p.150

currency against reality.'[13]

On the basis that it would defeat speculators and provide a stable environment for economic growth, John Smith won support for joining the ERM at the Labour conference in 1989; and on the 16 November 1989, at a meeting of the Shadow Cabinet, the new Labour economic orthodoxy was spelled out:

'The idea that the state could stimulate the economy, either by expanding the nationalised industries or through local councils, was out, [Shadow Chancellor] Smith told them. The government was not going to raise enough through taxes or borrowing because, other considerations aside, the rules of the ERM prevented it. This would mean... meeting industrial and financial leaders to *establish trus*t before election day. "We can leave dogmatism to the Tories," he said. So began the "prawn cocktail offensive..."'[14] (Emphasis added.)

It is worth spelling this out. To get elected, Labour's pollsters were telling them, they had to be more convincing on economic policy; chiefly they had to look more convincing on anti-inflation policy. People still perceived them as in the pockets of the unions; and still believed the inflation of the 1970s had been caused by Labour and their union allies. Despite the Tory inflation of the 1970s, followed by the Tory recession of the 1980s, people still perceived the Tories to be the party of economic competence – an astonishing indictment of the sheer political ineptitude of the Labour Party leadership.

As Bryan Gould pointed out, Labour's policy of supporting entry into the ERM, about which Mrs Thatcher was dragging her feet, actually meant that 'the City and other critics... need have no fears about inflation under a Labour Government since monetary policy would no longer be under the control of government. In fact it would be contracted out to an independent mecha-

[13] Guardian 19 August 1995. After the collapse of British membership of the ERM, Smith's biographer, Andy McSmith, claims that the Labour front bench knew that the 2.95 D-mark/sterling rate was too high for sterling to enter the ERM, but they said nothing for fear of the effect on the pound. That is, they were afraid they would achieve what they, apparently, thought was the right thing: a lower pound! Aah, politics...

[14] McSmith p. 161. Smith was quoted in The Sunday Times 1 March 1992: 'Labour policy was quick to be ahead of the game with ERM entry which the City liked.'

nism.'[15] The City liked the ERM because to maintain sterling at a fixed position within the ERM would entail keeping interest rates high, just as it had done in the 60s with fixed exchange rates, 'to maintain the value of the pound'. The chief consequence of keeping interest rates high would be a depressed domestic economy; and so, voila! low inflation – and good times for the City of London as high interest rates attracted the world's speculative money. In effect, Labour's leaders had decided that the City was too powerful to oppose.

THE KILLING OF CRUSTACEANS BEGINS

The 'prawn cocktail offensive' saw members of the Shadow Cabinet, especially John Smith and Marjorie Mowlem, touring the dining-rooms of the City of London assuring their hosts that, despite the destruction of the British economy they had caused in the previous decade, and despite their role in some of the biggest rip-offs in British history, Labour had no intention of making their lives any less profitable than they had been under Mrs Thatcher.

John Smith's 'establishing trust' turned out to mean, 'Trust us, we will do nothing you do not approve of; we will support membership of the EEC and the ERM.' At one such meeting, 'International currency dealers were promised there would be no attempt to bring back exchange controls. That genie is out of the bottle, Smith declared.'[16] At another, Smith's biographer, Andy McSmith, without a trace of irony that I can detect, describes John Smith getting an ovation from an audience of bankers for announcing that Labour did not intend to nationalise the banks – something which had not been seriously considered in the previous fifty years![17] Stuart Bell MP went to New York on a trip paid for by Kleinwort Benson Securities, to reassure Wall Street that the 'financial markets will be safe in the hands of a future Labour Government'.[18] Calling it an 'offensive' was a nice bit of spinning:

[15] Ibid.

[16] Guardian (Dairy) 26 October 1995

[17] Some of its personnel are listed in 'Labour's Friends in the City', Sunday Telegraph (Business) 1 March 1992.

[18] Some are listed in 'Love in a gold climate', Sunday Telegraph magazine 17 December 1995. The group is also discussed in 'Business Butters Up Blair', Sunday Telegraph (Business) 29 September 1996.

it would have been more accurately named the prawn cocktail surrender.

BUSINESS BEGINS SIGNING UP WITH LABOUR

A number of the forums at which Labour politicians met representatives of business and finance were expanded or created as the good news spread that the sectors of British capital which supported membership of the EEC now had new champions. The older Labour Finance and Industry Group doubled its membership between 1990 and 1992.[19] In 1993 the Industry Forum was set up by Gerald Frankel, who had been a Deputy Chair of the Labour Finance and Industry Group. By December 1995 it had 150 members.[20] Unlike the Labour Finance and Industry Group which had some well-established roots in the Labour Party, Frankel's Industry Forum was simply a mechanism through which firms gave money to the Labour Party. Among the large companies to join it were Thorn EMI, Glaxo Wellcome, Alfred McAlpine, NatWest, Nissan, AT&T and Hambros bank.[21] In August 1995 Frankel sponsored an 'initiative' in which City figures sought to persuade the Labour Party that it was mistaken in its belief that the City was obsessed with short-termism, a belief which, said Frankel, 'was prejudicing dialogue between Labour and the City.'[22] Clearly, 'trust' had not yet been established.[23]

The message of Labour's capitulation to the old orthodoxy was spread internationally: Gordon Brown and John Smith attended a meeting of the Bilderberg group in 1991. Though the 'offensive' failed to win the 1992 election, eventually Labour's surrender to the financial and overseas lobby paid off handsomely. By 1995 the

[19] Daily Telegraph 14 August 1995

[20] Guardian 25 August 1995.

[21] Another, but relatively insignificant group, was the Smithfield discussion group, led by John Norton, a banker, who subsequently married Marjorie Mowlem, who had been a part of the 'prawn cocktail offensive'. See '150 City members meet regularly in the crypt of St Mary le Bow,' Sunday Times March 1 1992. In the article Mowlem is said to have eaten 150 City lunches in 18 months.

[22] 'George welcomes Labour proposals' (Guardian 22 May 1995); 'Bankers woo Opposition as Tories slump in the polls' (Guardian 25 August 1995); 'Tory MP tells City to cultivate Labour' (Guardian 16 June 1995); 'City warms to Labour's stance on the Bank' (Independent 2 May 1995) to cite just a few of the headlines.

[23] Ranelagh p. 261

financial pages of the newspapers were full of articles in praise of Labour's policies.[24]

The Labour Party leadership had concluded that the only way to get elected was to accept the agenda of the Americans and the City, to be pro-NATO, pro-nuclear, pro-EEC, pro-free markets and pro-non regulation of the City. The strategy might have succeeded on its own but it was guaranteed success by Mrs Thatcher's increasing hostility to European integration and the ERM during this period. Without that, without the fear that the Conservative Party might turn out to be anti-EEC, the City and the rest of the overseas lobby would not have given their approval to Labour.

It is curious that it turned out to be Mrs Thatcher, the woman who grew up in the corner shop, the apparent champion of the small business and the entrepreneur, the English nationalist, who should oversee the decimation of British manufacturing – 'her people' – by the trans-national interests of the City of London. Was it simply that, like most other people, she never saw that there was conflict between industry and the City, between the domestic economy and the overseas lobby? Did she simply share the 'assumption that the interests of the City were identical to those of the country'?[25] I suspect she did; not least because this kind of perception of the economy and society is just absent from Conservative thinking. And though her memoirs give us no clues, every so often there have been glimpses of another Thatcher, generally concealed from the public gaze.

THE REAL MRS THATCHER?

In their biography Wapshot and Brock note in the 1960s that Mrs Thatcher 'showed a noticeable bias against the City in favour of business interests – a not unusual rhetorical stance among many leading Conservatives of the time.'[26] In 1981 an article in The Guardian headed 'Are the banks to blame?', included this:

'At a pre-budget lunch with the Committee of London Clearing Bankers, top executives were unable to get a word in, so persistently did she lecture them on their shortcomings... Mrs Thatcher's attitude is usually traced to her displeasure at the role of the banks in the sudden expansion of lending last year when

---

[25] Guardian, 16 September, 1981.

[26] Sunday Telegraph, 3 January, 1988.

"corset" controls were removed, undermining money supply policy... the uncannily similar background of an explosion of bank lending to the personal sector which is already being likened by some City analysts to the Barber boom of the early 1970s.'[27]

In 1988, The Sunday Telegraph carried a piece headed 'Honours snub to City is resented', which began:

'There is growing unease in the City of London at an apparent snub meted out in the New Year's Honours list in the year of "Big Bang"... back-bench MPs with City backgrounds are upset at what they see as a calculated example of Mrs Thatcher's dislike for the money markets and the businessmen who work in them...' An unidentified Tory MP was quoted as saying that, "The Prime Minister has long been disenchanted with the City. She feels that it is politically inept and that it could have been much more helpful over the government's BP share rescue operation which, after all, bailed the brokers out. Mrs Thatcher is also known to disapprove of the high salaries some City businessmen have been paid since Big Bang."'[28]

In his memoir Nigel Lawson comments that 'Margaret had no love for the banks'.[29] In his fascinating account of the rise of Thatcherism, written from a seat inside the Conservative Central Office, John Ranelagh comments that Mrs Thatcher was 'not sanguine about... the shift in Britain from manufacturing to service industries;'[30] and as described in chapter 6, she tried unsuccessfully to change the basis of monetary policy in the pursuit of lower interest rates.

Partly it was just politics. The Conservative Party is a coalition of interests and beliefs. The fragments above suggest that Thatcher wasn't just a simple-minded English nationalist who

---

[27] p. 93

[28] p. 245

[29] Ranelagh p. 260

[30] Alan Walters subsequently wrote of a campaign to 'get' him. This theme emerged in baroque form on April 10 1990, when A.V. R. Smith, the Western Goals Institute's Executive Director, referred to a 'conspiracy to undermine the Prime Minister... the determination of the financial oligarchy to STOP THATCHER AT ALL COSTS.' (Emphasis in original.) It was in a letter accompanying a Western Goals' Viewpoint Paper, 'Hit-job on Margaret Thatcher', which traced her troubles to the 1989 Bilderberg meeting and her refusal to endorse the plans for an independent European Central Bank. (cont. overleaf)

bought the City of London's 'line'; more that the English nationalist Thatcher was also a practical politician. Having been defeated by the Treasury-Bank of England-City axis in 1980/81, when she was still a new and relatively weak leader of the Tory Party with a Cabinet containing a large number of her opponents, she accepted the financial sector (and economic policy) as off-limits. She did nothing, for example, in the years when Chancellor Nigel Lawson was 'shadowing' the D-mark, a policy she opposed. (Her subsequent claims that she was unaware of Lawson's policy are preposterous.) Her memoirs portray someone trying to swim against the European tide but unwilling – or unable – to actually resist it. It was only when the issue of the UK joining the European Monetary System (EMS), as a step towards European Monetary Union, came to a head that the nationalist in her reappeared. The result was that:

'... for the first time, Margaret Thatcher appeared to be colliding with the City, and thus with some of the people whom she had "made" during the previous decade... [she] was now acting against joining the EMS which the City, anxious to maintain its centrality as a dispenser of services, wanted to join... interests which she did a great deal to create and to sustain were finding her not so useful any more.' [31]

THATCHER AGAINST THE EURO-TIDE

This conflict took the form of a symbolic struggle between her economic advisor, Alan Walters, who had returned to the fold in May 1989, and the official economic policy organisations, led by Nigel Lawson, then Chancellor. Just as it was with Monetary Base Control in 1980/81, discussed in chapter 6, it was Thatcher plus

[30 cont.] Certainly there was a conflict between Thatcher, the nationalist, and the trans-national, globalising forces attempting, through the idea of European unity and the mechanism of the independent European bank, to impose on the (as was then) European Community members the hegemony of finance re-established in Britain in the 1980s. But Western Goals were simply wrong to see this directly linked to groups like the Bilderbergers and the Trilateralists, as if such groups functioned as executive committees of trans-national capitalism. There is little evidence that this is the case. What there is is in Mike Peters' essay on Bilderberg in Lobster 32. They are more agenda-setting and consensus-seeking.

[31] Not that she did anything. The great patriot actually spent the first part of the war in school and then, in 1943, she went to university.

unofficial advisors against the rest of the Whitehall economics apparatus. And once again she lost.[32] In the end Mrs Thatcher was removed by her Conservative colleagues who feared that she was going to lose them the election; and the major component of that was not monetary policy, let alone the ERM, but the Poll Tax, which very definitely was hers.

Mrs Thatcher is of the generation who lived through the Second World War, and it was her ally, the late Nicholas Ridley, who said in 1990 that the EMS was a 'German racket'. (He might have added, just like the British racket – the sterling area – before it.) So she made her famous speech at Bruges opposing the movement towards European integration but she had already signed the Single European Act which paved the way for European federation. The account of this in her memoir is bizarre. Quoting the Single European Act's 'objective of progressive realisation of economic and monetary union' she comments:

'I was more or less happy with this, because it meant no more than co-operation. The rest of the European heads of government were equally happy, because they interpreted it as progress towards towards a European Central Bank and a single currency.' (p. 741)

Like Humpty Dumpty or Alice In Wonderland, Mrs Thatcher was saying, 'When I use a word, it means just what I choose it to mean – neither more nor less.' In the ensuing struggle over European policy she lost from her cabinet, in rapid succession, Nigel Lawson and Geoffrey Howe, the original political architects of City hegemony, and finally resigned. This ending to her career might have been avoided. She could have faced down the Cabinet, sacked a few, openly and publicly rejected the ERM, and appealed to the nationalist sentiments in the English – and I mean English, not British – voter. It might have worked, who can say? It has never actually been tried by anyone in such a leadership position. At any rate, she could have gone down fighting. Instead, she gave in – just as she had done in 1981 over Monetary Base Control. But she left behind her a transformed Labour Party, once again pro-American, pro-NATO, pro-nuclear, pro-free market, pro-

---

[32] 'The party, having plumped for the ERM partly because Margaret Thatcher was against it, allowed the tactic to be a substitute for policy.' Rintoul p. 267.

overseas lobby; and, in large part thanks to her opposition to them, pro-EEC and pro-ERM. Under Mrs Thatcher the Tories had ceased to be a safe bet to do what the overseas lobby wanted – and into that role stepped the Labour Party.

[2] The interests and views of the non-European Union overseas interests are best reflected in the pages of The Sunday Telegraph and largely, though not entirely, explain why that paper is so hostile to the European Union.

[3] OECD figures from Larry Elliot, Guardian Economics Editor, in The Guardian 15 July 1996.

Chapter Eight

UNCLE SAM AND NEW LABOUR

'The New Labour project has always been defined in an Anglo-American context.'[1]

Gordon Brown used to tell interviewers that he spent his summer holidays in the library at Harvard University. In 1986, CND member Tony Blair went on one of those US-sponsored trips to America that are available for promising MPs and came back a supporter of the nuclear deterrent.[2] Blair, Brown and John Monks, an important Blair ally as head of the TUC, have all attended meetings of the Bilderberg group, one of the meeting places of the European-American trans-national elite.[3]

David Miliband, Blair's head of policy, did a Masters degree at the Massachusetts Institute of Technology.[4]

Jonathan Powell, Blair's foreign policy adviser, is a former

[1] Martin Kettle, the Guardian 3 February 1996

[2] The Observer 14 April 1996. This visit is missing from John Rentouls' biography of Blair, Tony Blair, (Little Brown, London, 1995).

[3] Gordon Brown, with the late John Smith, attended the 1991 meeting at Baden-Baden. (This is not included in his 1998 biography by Paul Routledge.) The full list of those attending was published in the US magazine The Spotlight 22 July 1991. This article with others from the same source on the Bilderberg group and Trilateral Commission can be found on the Net at http://www.real.net.au/insurge/politics/global_power/nword.htm/ The Spotlight is undoubtedly a racist magazine. Nonetheless it is the only magazine which consistently prints articles about trans-national forums like Bilderberg and Trilateral. Monks attended the meeting in 1996. The list of those attending the 1996 meeting was published in Canada and then put up on the Net. Tony Blair's Bilderberg meeting is in his Parliamentary declaration of interests.

[4] The Guardian 3 October 1994

Foreign Office official whose previous posting was in the British Embassy in Washington.[5] Edward Balls, Gordon Brown's economics adviser, studied at Harvard, wrote editorials for The Financial Times, and was about to join the World Bank before he joined Brown.[6] His wife, 1997 MP Yvette Cooper, also studied at Harvard. Sue Nye, Gordon Brown's personal assistant, lives with Gavyn Davies, chief economist with the American bankers, Goldman Sachs, and one of Labour's chief economic advisers.[7] Marjorie Mowlam, now Secretary of State for Northern Ireland, did a PhD at the University of Iowa and then taught in the United States in the 1970s.[8] Chris Smith, now Heritage Minister, was a Kennedy Scholar in the USA – as were David Miliband and Ed Balls.[9]

And then there's Peter Mandelson, Blair's confidant, chief strategist and, as this was being written, Minister without Portfolio. By the end of his final year at Oxford University in 1976, via the United Nations Association, Mandelson had become Chair of British Youth Council.[10] The British Youth Council began as the British section of the World Assembly of Youth (WAY), which was

[5] Ken Coates and Michael Barett Brown suggest in their book The Blair Revelation (Spokesman, Nottingham, 1996) that Powell's job in the British embassy in Washington concealed a role as the liaison officer between British intelligence and the CIA, but they have no evidence. Powell's career summary as given in The Diplomatic Service List for 1995 contains nothing from which to directly infer an intelligence role. He was born in 1956 and joined the FCO (Foreign and Commonwealth Office) in 1979. Since then he was Third later Second Secretary in Lisbon, 1981; Second later First Secretary at the FCO, London; UK delegate to CDE Stockholm 1986; UK delegate at the CSCE in Vienna 1986; First Secretary FCO, London 1989; then First Secretary (Chancery) Washington 1991.

[6] The Guardian 3 October 1994. Balls was profiled in the Guardian (G2) 16 March 1998.

[7] The Sunday Telegraph 24 March 1996. Davies was an adviser to the Callaghan Government as a member of the Downing Street Policy Unit, headed by (now Sir) Bernard Donoghue. He was included in the party which visited President Clinton in early 1998.

[8] Who's Who 1992

[9] Peter Hennessy, 'The View from Here', in The Independent (Education) 1 May 1997

[10] Mandelson 'flunked first year exams because he was spending all his time working as president of the United Nations Association's youth and student branch.' Independent 1 July 1989.

set up and financed by the CIA and SIS in the early 1950s to combat the Soviet Union's youth fronts.[11] By Mandelson's time in the mid-1970s – under a Labour Government – the British Youth Council was said to be financed by the Foreign Office, though that may have been a euphemism for SIS. Peter Mandelson, we were told in 1995 by Donald McIntyre in The Independent, is 'a pillar of the two blue-chip foreign affairs think-tanks, Ditchley Park and Chatham House.'[12]

Peter Mandelson, Marjorie Mowlam, Defence Minister George Robertson, Heritage Minister Chris Smith, and junior Foreign Office Minister in the House of Lords, Elizabeth Symons, are all members of the British-American Project for a Successor Generation (BAP), the latest in the long line of American-funded networks which promote American interests among the British political élite.[13] The BAP newsletter for June/July 1997 headlined its account of the May 1997 General Election, 'Big Swing to BAP'.

An older and more direct expression of American influence within the wider British labour movement is the Trade Union Committee for European and Transatlantic Understanding (TUCETU). TUCETU is the successor to the Labour Committee for Transatlantic Understanding (LCTU), which was set up in 1976 by the late Joe Godson, Labour Attaché at the US embassy in London in the 1950s who, as discussed above, had become an intimate of the then leader of the party, Hugh Gaitskell.

Organised by two officials of the NATO-sponsored Atlantic Council, TUCETU incorporates Peace Through NATO, the group central to Michael Heseltine's MoD campaign against CND in the early 1980s, and receives over £100,000 a year from the Foreign Office.

TUCETU chair Alan Lee Williams was a Labour defence minister in the Callaghan Government, before he defected to the SDP; director Peter Robinson runs the National Union of Teachers'

[11] On WAY see the scattering of references in Joel Kotek's Students and the Cold War, (Macmillan, London 1996), Joseph B. Smith, Portrait of a Cold Warrior, (Ballantine, New York 1981) and Jonathan Bloch and Patrick Fitzgerald, British Intelligence and Covert Action, (Junction, London 1983).

[12] The Independent 29 July 1995. McIntyre is reported (1998) to be writing a biography of Mandelson.

[13] See Tom Easton's 'The British American Project for the Successor Generation', in Lobster 33.

education centre at Stoke Rochford near Grantham. In the mid-1980s Williams and Robinson were members of the european policy group of the Washington Center for Strategic and International Studies.

Among the senior union and Labour Party figures on the TUCETU's 1995 notepaper were Doug McAvoy, general secretary of the National Union of Teachers; CPSA general secretary Barry Reamsbottom (a member of the Successor Generation Project discussed above) and president Marion Chambers; Lord Richard, Labour leader in the House of Lords; former trade union leaders Bill Jordan (now head of the International Confederation of Free Trade Unions, the CIA's chief cold war labour movement operation),[14] Lord (Eric) Hammond, and Lord (Frank) Chapple.[15]

The Atlantic Council/TUCETU network provided New Labour's Ministry of Defence team. Defence Secretary George Robertson was a member of the Council of the Atlantic Committee from 1979-90; Lord Gilbert, Minister of State for Defence Procurement, is listed as TUCETU vice chair; Dr John Reid, Minister of State for the Armed Forces, spoke at a TUCETU conference; and MoD press office biographical notes on junior Defence Minister John Speller state that he 'has been a long standing member of the Trade Union Committee for European and Transatlantic Understanding'. Peter Mandelson has written a (very dull) pamphlet for TUCETU based on a speech he gave to its 1996 conference.

In other words, the people round Blair, the key New Labour 'project' personnel, are all linked to the United States, or the British foreign policy establishment, whose chief aim, since the end of the Second World War, has been to preserve the Anglo-American 'special relationship' to compensate for long-term economic decline.

WE ASKED THE AMERICANS...

Mr Blair has been quite open about the US role in all this. To the annual conference of Rupert Murdoch's News Corp he said:

'...the Americans have made it clear they want a special rela-

---

[14] On which see, for example 'The AFL-CIA' in Frazier (ed.) and Peter E. Newell, 'The International Centre of Free Trade Unionists in Exile' in Lobster 31.

[15] These paragraphs on TUCETU are taken from David Osler's 'American and Tory Intervention in the British Unions since the 1970's' in Lobster 33.

tionship with Europe, not with Britain alone. If we are to be listened to seriously in Washington or Tokyo, or the Pacific, we will often be acting with the rest of Europe... the Labour Government I hope to lead will be outward-looking, internationalist and committed to free and open trade, not an outdated and misguided narrow nationalism.'[16]

It could hardly be more specific: we asked the Americans and they said go with Europe and free trade. In other words, go with traditional, post-war American foreign policy objectives; and, since the mid-1960s, the objectives of the British overseas lobby. Put another way: thanks to the massive exportation of British capital which began during the Thatcher years, British-based capital has the largest overseas investments after America, and we will continue to support American political and military hegemony as the best protection for those interests. This is being 'outward-looking' – looking beyond Britain to where British capital has gone.

But British economic policy being 'outward-looking, internationalist and committed to free and open trade', in Blair's words, is precisely the problem from which non-metropolitan Britain has suffered for most of this century. These are the values of the overseas lobby, the Home Counties financial élite, people for whom Hull or Norwich, let alone Glasgow and Cardiff, are far away places about which they know nothing – and care about as much.

The analysis of the Gould group – and that of the many other similar analyses which preceded it – implied that Labour, if it sought acceptability from British capitalism, should look to the domestic economy, to a more radical version of the producers' alliance attempted by the governments of Wilson, Callaghan and Heath.

But John Smith and Marjorie Mowlem did not embark on a tour of the regional offices of the CBI, or the Chambers of Commerce of the British cities. They headed for the Square Mile. The Blairites, following the lead of John Smith, have become the party of the City, the big trans-national corporations and the Foreign Office – the overseas lobby.

They have become the party of the Europe Union – British membership of which is still supported by a majority of the over-

[16] The Times 17 July 1995.

seas lobby in Britain.[17] This shift explains the enthusiasm for the Blair faction expressed by the London establishment – the Foreign Office, the higher media and the EU-oriented section of British capital – in the run-up to the General Election of 1997. Labour under the Blair faction was a more reliable bet for continued EU membership than the Conservative Party with its vociferous Euro-sceptic wing.[18] And with this shift to an overseas orientation, comes the concomitant position that Labour's traditional constituency – so-called Old Labour – the domestic economy, especially manufacturing and the public sector, becomes merely a collection of special interest groups to be taken for granted, conned, betrayed or ignored.

THE PROBLEM BECOMES THE SOLUTION

The key move was to see the City – the overseas lobby – and the asset-stripping of the domestic economy, which began in the 1980s, not as the problem but as the solution. This shift can be illustrated by two quotations. The first is from the Labour Party policy document, Meet the Challenge Make the Change: A new agenda for Britain, the final report of Labour's Policy Review for the 1990s, published in 1989. The sub-section Finance for Industry (p. 13), began:

'Under-investment is the most obvious symptom of short-termism in our economic affairs, yet there is no shortage of funds for investment purposes. The problem lies in the criteria by which the City judges investment opportunities. If short-termism is the disease, then it is the City which is the source of the infection.'

This section is a rewrite by what Austin Mitchell MP called 'the leadership'[19] of a section of the document written by the committee chaired by Bryan Gould. The original Gould committee version had stated, inter alia :

'The concentration of power and wealth in the City of London

[17] The non-EU section of overseas UK capital, located chiefly in the US, the Commonwealth and the Republic of South Africa, is less enthusiastic about EU membership. Their views are expressed most clearly in the Sunday Telegraph.

[18] An unnamed 'businessman close to the Labour leadership' said in the Observer (Business)13 April 1997, p. 5: 'The big companies - the ones who do the most trading with Europe - are really worried about the xenophobe right.'

[19] See his review of Defeat from the Jaws of Victory: Inside Kinnock's Labour Party by Heffernan and Maquesee, in the Guardian 15 December 1992.

is the major cause of Britain's economic problems'; and that Britain's economic policy had for too long 'been dominated by City values and run in the interests of those who hold assets rather than those who produce.'[20]

Seven years later in their The Blair Revolution, Peter Mandelson and co-author Roger Liddle, now Tony Blair's adviser on Europe, said of Britain in the 1990s:

'Britain can boast of some notable economic strengths – for example, the resilience and high internationalisation of our top companies, our strong industries like pharmaceuticals, aerospace, retailing and media; the pre-eminence of the City of London.'[21]

Not only has the City ceased to be the problem it was perceived to be nine years before, Mandelson and Liddle have internalised the values of the overseas sector of the economy, of which the City is the core. Not only is the 'high internationalisation' of our top companies an 'economic strength', we now have a retailing 'industry' and media 'industry'.

GOODBYE MANUFACTURING

As we saw in chapter 4, the prospect of North Sea oil revenues had begun to persuade members of the overseas lobby that they could, perhaps, abandon what they saw as the troublesome, union-ridden, manufacturing sector of the economy. In 1978, we learn from Frank Blackaby, that a 'senior Treasury official' had commented, 'Perhaps we can either have North Sea oil or manufacturing industry, but not both.'[22] On 3 July 1980, Samuel Brittan, who was then the leading economic commentator on the right of British politics, published an article in The Financial Times headed, 'Deindustrialisation is good for the UK.'

The former Thatcher Minister, the late Nicholas Ridley, wrote in his memoir:

'I do not think it is a disaster if we become an economy based

[20] Cited in Eric Shaw's 'The Evolution of Labour's Campaign Strategy 1987-91: some Preliminary Notes and Comments', a paper presented at the Conference of the Political Studies Association, Queen's University, Belfast 7-9 April 1992. Thanks to John Booth for this.

[21] Faber and Faber, 1996, p. 12

[22] Frank Blackaby, 'Exchange Rate Policy and Economic Strategy' in Three Banks Review, June 1980.

primarily on the service sector. It isn't vital, as socialists seem to think, that we have a large manufacturing sector. They seem to think this mainly because Britain's old manufacturing industries used to be the basis of their political support.'[23]

The former Conservative Minister, Cecil Parkinson, one of Mrs Thatcher's Ministers at the Department of Trade and Industry, wrote in his memoir:

'Trade [i.e. Ministry for Trade at the DTI] traditionally took the view that it was the custodian of GATT and upholder of the open market wherever possible. It tried to ensure that we acted within the rules of GATT and was sometimes regarded as almost unpatriotic when it argued the case that just because other people's imports were unwelcome this was not necessarily unfair.'[24]

Whereas a domestically-oriented Department of Trade might see its role as promoting British exports, defining its role as the 'the upholder of the open market' is as clear an expression of the overseas lobby's views as can be imagined.

As the Thatcher regime accelerated the deindustrialisation of Britain, this was rationalised in and around the City of London and by some of its spokespersons in the Tory Party, notably Chancellor of the Exchequer Nigel Lawson, with the belief that financial and other services would replace manufacturing industry: we were moving to a post-industrial society, such as... Switzerland?[25]

During John Major's period as Prime Minister, Edward Pearce wrote:

'I have been told by a Treasury knight that though very fond of Mr Major, he worried a little at his anxiety about manufacturers. "He wasn't very happy with the analogies we made about Switzerland, so prosperous entirely from service industries, so it was necessary to let him make friendly things (sic) to the manufacturing people."'[26]

---

[23] Ridley p. 71

[24] Parkinson pp. 238 and 9

[25] In the 1000 plus pages of Nigel Lawson's memoir, there are only four indexed references to the manufacturing sector, in the last of which he comments that if North Sea oil has 'crowded out' manufacturing, then as North Sea oil declines, it will spontaneously 'crowd back in'. See p. 196.

[26] Guardian 8 January 1992

Pearce is telling us that one of the most senior civil servants at the Treasury, and by implication – the use of 'we' – perhaps several or all of them, had decided that Britain should pursue a policy of abandoning its manufacturing base altogether.[27]

One of Gordon Brown's appointments to the Bank of England Monetary Policy Committee, the American economist DeAnne Julius, was the co-author of an essay which argued that it would be a mistake for Western governments to try and hang on to their manufacturing base and that they should concentrate on service industries.[28] (And according to William Keegan in the Observer 15 February 1998, Ms Julius is 'widely considered to be the closest the MPC [Monetary Policy Committee] has to someone in touch with industry'!)

Such attitudes are now openly expressed in the financial media. Gavyn Davies is perhaps Labour's most important economic advisor. He lives with Gordon Brown's office manager, Sue Nye, and is the chief economist for the US bank Goldman Sachs. Immediately after the Labour election victory in 1997 he dismissed concern about the damage the rising pound was doing to British exporters, with the comment that 'the health of the one sector of the economy which is directly affected by the exchange rate [i.e. domestic manufacturing] cannot take precedence over the maintenance of the inflation target.'[29] (Davies' implied claim that the City is not 'directly affected by the exchange rate' is an extraordinary lie or self-delusion. The higher it is the more money the City makes.) By early 1998 Davies' response had become the standard reply to all complaints about the value of sterling.

The same line was offered in The Daily Telegraph in 1998 in an article whose title, 'Metal bashers shut up shop and do the nation a service', echoed that of Samuel Brittan's 'De-industrialisation is good for Britain' nearly twenty years before:

'Sympathy for manufacturers is no basis for economic

[27] The 'Treasury knights' are the Permanent Secretaries. I asked Pearce who he was quoting but while he did not identify the Treasury official, he commented: 'I'm pretty sure that factory-despising attitudes are common in the Treasury though not universal.' Letter to author 14 January 1992.

[28] See Nick Cohen's 'Why is CIA ex-agent setting our interest rates?' in The Observer 19 October 1997. Ms Julius, now with British Airways, worked as an analyst for the CIA.

[29] The Independent 12 May 1997

policy...the plain fact is that manufacturing will go on shrinking, and the more prosperous we become, the faster it will decline...interest rates may be relatively high, but setting them in order to succour manufacturing will only succeed in feeding inflation.'[30]

With these attitudes comes the extension of the term 'industry' to encompass any kind of economic activity. We now have 'service industries', 'financial industries', 'leisure industries', 'the sports industry', 'the tourism industry', 'the gambling industry', 'the sex industry' etc. etc. It does not matter if the manufacture of products in Britain declines: they will continue to be replaced by financial 'products', holiday 'products', leisure 'products' and so forth. (As yet I haven't noticed welfare 'products' but they cannot be far off now.)

New Labour's economic policy makes no distinction between the City and domestic manufacturing. But policies which suit the domestic economy – cheap money, expansion, controls on the uses of money and credit; planning, consistent demand in the economy – do not suit the City which wants expensive money (sorry: 'competitive interest rates') and freedom from controls (sorry: 'self regulation'). This used to be understood by the Labour Party and was the basis of party economic policy until the mid 1980s.[31]

New Labour still occasionally recognises that there is something called the domestic manufacturing economy.

As the value of sterling rose throughout the first year of New Labour's first term in government with the steady dose of increase rate rises imposed by the newly independent Bank of England, government spokespersons initially watched from the wings and made ritual noises of sympathy and regret – what the unnamed Treasury official quoted above called 'making friendly things to the manufacturing people.'

• 'Mr Brown ... is concerned that sterling's 20% appreciation over the past 12 months will damage industry by making exports more expensive.'[32]

• Helen Liddell, Economic Secretary to the Treasury: 'We share

[30] 7 February 1998

[31] See for example Neil Kinnock's Making Our Way (Blackwell, 1986)

[32] Guardian 7 July 1997

the concern about the impact the pound has on industry.'[33]

• President of the Board of Trade, Margaret Beckett: 'The Government values the manufacturing base of this country and shares its belief in the benefits of a stable and competitive exchange rate.'[34]

But three months later Mrs Beckett told the annual dinner of the Engineering Employers' Federation that the government 'has to take a view of across the whole economy, not just a part, even as important a part as manufacturing' – the line offered by Gavyn Davies, quoted above.[35]

A FATAL INVERSION?

British politics has been stood on its head. The Conservative Party, traditionally the party of financial and overseas interests, has been replaced in that role by Labour. Instructed by its new friends in the City, Labour has become the party of financial, pre-Keynesian, orthodoxy. Gordon Brown looks determined to re-enact the role of Philip Snowden in 1931 – the perfect Labour Party front man for the interests of the overseas lobby. The last three years of the Major regime saw Chancellor Kenneth Clarke running the kind of orthodox demand management policy – increasing government deficits in response to the recession – which Labour, under Wilson or Callaghan, would have run, but which is anathema to 'Iron Chancellor' Brown.

On becoming Chancellor, virtually his first action was to make the Bank of England independent; and the Bank of England said, 'Thanks very much' and began putting interest rates up, despite the pound being too high for the domestic manufacturing economy. The first year of New Labour's term of office produced a stream of newspaper stories complaining of the damage being done to British manufacturing by the strength of sterling identical to those which appeared in the first years of Mrs Thatcher's Government – and for the same reason: interest rates were being put up.[36] Once again, just as in the first years of the Thatcher

[33] Guardian 11 July 1997

[34] Guardian 5 December 1997

[35] Guardian 18 February 1998. She repeated this central 'line' in an exchange of letters with Austin Mitchell MP. See Larry Elliot, the Guardian 9 March 1998.

[36] See, for example, the leader 'Manufacturing a recession' in the Guardian 20 January 1998.

regime, the exchange rate for sterling was not a consideration.

Gordon Brown gave up the state's influence on the Bank of England, as far as we can tell, in the belief that independent central banks have a better record on preventing inflation than those under political control.[37] Which is another way of saying that, without prioritising the effects on the domestic economy, central banks can be relied on to put interest rates up. Gordon Brown acts as though he's got the equivalent of economic amnesia, and cannot remember anything that happened before 1997. How else can we explain his determination to try to 'control' inflation using only interest rates – what Edward Heath used to dismiss as 'one club golf' – and ignoring the large range of other economic tools which were used, in the days before Mrs Thatcher?

WE ARE POWERLESS

'New Labour' believes – but is unwilling to state in so many words – that governments can do nothing against the power of transnational finance. This belief has become the acid test for 'New Labour'. In the Commons debate on the Nick Leeson-Barings debacle on 27 February 1996, it was Sir Peter Tapsell, a High Tory stockbroker, not Shadow Chancellor Gordon Brown or Labour's City spokesman Alastair Darling, who declared that the derivatives market was 'so speculative in nature as to deserve the term gambling and perhaps should be banned in international law.'

Gordon Brown meekly echoed Chancellor of the Exchequer Kenneth Clarke and called for an inquiry. In a letter to me on the subject of Tapsell's remarks on derivatives, Alastair Darling, now Chief Secretary to the Treasury, made the following assertions:

'It is not possible to ban derivatives. They have been about for 200 or 300 years. Properly controlled and supervised there nothing per se wrong with them. The fault lies in the control systems. In any event, I trust that you will accept that it would be impossible for one country to ban the trade even it it was desirable. The trade would need to be banned throughout the world.'

To the implicit question, 'Why not do something about this?' Darling replied:

[37] See, for example, the arguments by Labour economics adviser Gavyn Davies, in The Independent 12 May 1997, and the replies in the Letters on 14 May.

It cannot be done. (So do nothing.) In any case, there is nothing wrong with them. (So do nothing.) Even if there was, and you wanted to ban them, it would have to be done world-wide. (So do nothing.)

The financial sector's interest in not being controlled by government has been universalised into the beliefs that not only is it impossible to impose such control, it is positively a bad thing to try. (The market is magic.) In an article in The Times, Peter Riddell said what the politicians never quite dare to say: 'Politicians know that real power lies with global business'. But where is the evidence to support this belief? Where is the evidence to support the view that the nation state can no longer manage its own economy?

When you ask you usually get told of the 'French failure' in 1983, when the Mitterand Government tried to expand the economy in a pretty traditional demand management fashion – while trying to remain a member of the European Monetary System. But as an example of the impossibility of demand management in one economy, this example fails. Just as Heath did in 1972 with his expansion, the French government reached the point where they either floated the currency as the trade balance went into deficit, or abandoned the expansion. Pursuit of the geo-political competition with Germany inside the then EEC, the so-called 'franc fort' policy, proved more important, and the French government abandoned the expansion.[38] Thus, it is believed on all sides, did 'Keynesianism in one country' die. But even the most lumpen accounts of demand management economics acknowledge that it may be necessary to abandon attempts to maintain fixed parities if growth is pursued. (The real mystery of the French expansion in 1983 is how they thought they thought they could have expansion and 'franc fort'.)

But while the French failure looms large in the we-are-powerless Labour modernising mind, the experience of Britain leaving the ERM in 1992, does not. Yet what happened in 1992 when Britain was forced out of the ERM in 1992 by these 'global forces' we are supposed to fear so much? Dire consequences were predicted if the pound left the ERM, notably a massive increase

[38] On this see Seamus Milne, 'A French lesson for the left' in Tribune 26 March 1993.

in inflation. (Being in the ERM was claimed to be a guaranteed anti-inflation measure by both Labour and Conservative economics spokespersons.) The world's currency dealers concluded that, at D-mark 2.95, the pound was seriously overvalued – a view shared by a wide section of British economists and, we are led to believe, despite their silence on the subject at the time, the Labour Shadow Cabinet.[39] The Conservative Government tried to defend an unrealistic exchange rate by the usual means – giving the Bank of England's reserves away to speculators – and then recognised defeat.

The value of sterling fell, and none of the predictions of economic disaster turned out to be true. Inflation did not shoot up; domestic production expanded with the more competitive pound, exports expanded and unemployment fell. In direct refutation of everything Labour's economics spokespersons apparently believed, the relatively good economic position inherited by the Blair government in 1997 is a direct consequence of the British economy leaving the ERM.

In The Independent on Sunday of 15 January 1996, Alastair Darling, now Treasury Minister, was quoted as saying, 'It is not up to the government to say that the banks can only make so much profit.' It certainly used to be 'up to the government': even Geoffrey Howe imposed a windfall tax on the banks in 1981; but that was back in those far-off days before the Government handed power to set interest rates, perhaps the most powerful single economic tool and the surest means of regulating how much banks earn, to the people who stand to gain by putting them up! Just before the 1997 General Election Roy Hattersley wrote in his Guardian column of meeting one of the then Labour shadow economics team, who told him that in the new global economy it was not possible for a government to increase taxes.[40]

On his visit to the beleaguered Bill Clinton in February 1998, Tony Blair told Guardian journalist and long-time Blair ally, Martin

[39] Neil Kinnock's assistant at the time, Neil Stewart, commented that the reason Kinnock did not express his belief that pound was over-valued was, 'It's a dick-head says it before the Tories.' Rintoul p. 267.

[40] Hattersley declined to tell me the name of this person. My guess? Alastair Darling. This was an echo of Tony Blair's 1996 comment in Japan that, 'We also recognise that in a global economy… our tax rates need to be internationally as well as nationally competitive.' Blair p. 123

Kettle, of the 'five clear principles of the centre-left'. The first of these was:

'... stable management and economic prudence because of the global economy.'[41]

The acid test for Labour 'modernisers' has become how completely you accept the powerlessness thesis. The line sounds immediately plausible to those, like New Labour economics spokespersons, with little economic knowledge: it is what they keep reading in the newspapers and being told by their advisers from the City. The powerlessness thesis also has the advantage of being a popular line with Labour supporters of the European Union who can argue, as the Labour Party has done since it became Euro-enthusiasts, that we need Europe to control capital ('the speculators').

A decade ago Gordon Brown et al. believed that British membership of the ERM would do it; when that failed they concluded that only a single currency would do it. But the propositions that nation states are powerless against capital movements, or that the free market model is the only one possible (or successful) are immediately falsified by the experience of Norway, and the Asian variants on corporatist, producer alliance, restrictive, trade barrier and exchange control-laden, nationalist economies of the Far East. These so-called 'tiger' economies had developed and grown in defiance of Anglo-American free market theories.[42]

Why have New Labour adopted the powerlessness thesis? In part, it is simply that they are in the grip of theories; and like most people in the grip of theories they exclude information which might challenge them. The theories are reinforced by the fact that they are those currently approved of by their mentors in the United States and the British overseas lobby. In so far as alternative views are perceived, they are offered by people who for one

---

[41] Guardian 7 February 1998.

[42] This was written just before the 1998 collapse of the so-called Asian 'tiger' economies. As far as I can see the collapse is chiefly the result of those economies reducing the restrictions which used to exist, in pursuit of the western free market model, thus encouraging speculation (aka 'investment') by their domestic and Euro-American financial sectors - with the usual disastrous results. On Norway see Larry Elliot in the Guardian 6 April 1998.

reason or another, are regarded by New Labour as either discredited, such as the Labour Left, or beyond the pale, such as the Tory Europhobes. Thirdly, and most importantly, New Labour politicians like the belief that they are powerless against the world's financial markets.

Powerless as they are, a range of things that Labour leaders used to have try to deliver – growth, economic justice, redistribution – have ceased to be rational expectations of them. Nothing can be done short of the European-wide level; and maybe not even then.[43] Life is infinitely easier for Labour economic ministers when all they have to do is follow the City's line.

---

[43] General Secretary of the TUC, John Monks, called in 1996 for 'world works councils for each major international company', Guardian 31 January 1996. International capitalism did not noticeably tremble at this absurd prospect. Against the globalisation-nation-state-is-powerless thesis, see for example Martin Wolf 'Far From Powerless' in the Financial Times 13 May 1997; 'Grand National idea produces winners', Larry Ellliot, the Guardian 20 October 1997, 'Don't be fooled: multinationals do not rule the world', Independent on Sunday 12 January 1997 and 'Globaloney', Paul Hirst in Prospect February 1996.

Chapter Nine

LABOUR'S FEAR OF THE CITY

New Labour's leaders may now tell themselves that they are following the City's line in economic policy because they believe it to be correct, because the global free market is the best of all realistically possible worlds; because, in Mrs Thatcher's absurd dictum, there is no alternative. But the truth is they are following it because they are afraid of the City.

That fear is mostly the result of ignorance, coupled with – rationalised by – the unquestioned belief that the City is a major source of income for Britain and is thus 'a good thing'. From the days of the John Smith-Marjorie Mowlem 'prawn cocktail offensive' round the City's dining rooms to the general election campaign of 1997, Labour sought to reassure the Square Mile that it was going to be 'responsible' – i.e. leave them alone. Smith, Mowlem et al believed that the City could destroy a Labour Government it didn't approve of. But what could a hostile City actually do? There are three possibilities: they could leave London (much of the City is now foreign-owned); they could sell sterling and move into another currency – try to create a sterling crisis; or they could refuse to buy government debt, a 'gilt strike'.

Taking the third threat first: a politically-motivated gilt strike is impossible to operate in today's global financial world. If the return on the paper looks reasonable, someone will buy it. The second option need not detain us long. Currency speculators can only mount a political attack on a currency when attempts are made to maintain that currency at an inappropriate fixed exchange rate; as happened when the Tories tried to defend too high a sterling rate within the ERM in 1990-1992, or when Wilson tried to defend the $2.40 rate in the 1964-7 period. But with a floating currency, a pound irrationally driven down by speculation will be pushed back up by the global economy more interested in real factors: interest rates, GDP, deficits, growth. Of the three it is the threat that the money-men might leave London which has to be considered. This is a 'threat' because it is assumed that London's financial sector – including more than 500 foreign banks – is good for the British economy.

THE CITY IS GOOD FOR BRITAIN?

This is both highly debatable and difficult to debate because not only are there are no reliable figures, there is no agreement on what the various occupational and sectoral categories represent. I first began trying to collect figures on this in 1994. The then Treasury Secretary Anthony Nelson said in 1993 that banking and financial services accounted for over 10% of the GDP and earned over £4.4 billion for the balance of payments.[1]

But a year later, citing data from the London Business School, Bill Jamieson showed the financial sector's surplus in 1991 as £8 billion.[2] Other estimates – that is guesses – of Britain's 'invisible' surplus in this period ranged from £4-6 billion,[3] to the £15.6 billion claimed by the City propaganda group, British Invisibles in 1993.[4]

A year later this group had raised the figure to £20 billion.[5] Britain 1994: an official handbook claimed that 'British financial institutions' [undefined] overseas earnings amounted to £18,800 million in 1992'.[6] By 1997 the Guardian was quoting figures of £22.7 billion in 1996, double those of a decade ago.[7]

To muddle things further, a Treasury press release issued on 11 June 1996 and headed 'Competitiveness', went on to state that in 1994, 'the UK had the largest invisible surplus of almost 14 million dollars', and added that in 1995 it had fallen – halved! – to 7 billion

---

[1] The Daily Telegraph 4 January 1993

[2] The Sunday Telegraph , 6 February 1994

[3] Colin Harbury and Richard G. Lispey, An Introduction to the UK Economy, (Fourth Edition, Blackwell, 1993) pp. 246-7, figs 7.10 and 7.11.

[4] The Independent, 2 September 94

[5] The Sunday Telegraph, 24 September 1995

[6] HMSO, London, 1993, p. 178

[7] Made up of: banks £7.1 billion; insurance £6.1 billion; pension funds £2.3 billion. Guardian 11 July 1997, 'Export pendulum swings from industry to City.'

dollars![8] A month later, on 10 July, another Treasury press release announced that 'net overseas earnings of the UK financial services sector' was 20.4 billion pounds.

In a piece on Labour's new acceptance of the City, the Guardian of 4 October 1994 reported that the financial sector 'now generates one fifth of Britain's national income'. When I inquired of the journalists concerned about the source of the figures, they referred me to Labour's then City spokesperson, Alastair Darling. His office quoted the 1994 Central Statistical Office Blue Book (UK National Accounts) to the effect that 'net income generated by financial intermediation, real estate, renting and business activities' amounted to 18.5% of GDP. But 18.5% is not 'one fifth'; and that 18.5% includes activities a good deal wider than those meant by 'the financial sector', or 'the City'.

Labour MP Mike O'Brien, Darling's successor as Shadow Economic Secretary with special responsibility for City affairs, was quoted as saying in 1996 that the City, not the more complex category offered by Darling's office, produced 18 per cent of GDP and rising.[9] In 1998 a survey by British Invisibles announced that the financial services sector 'accounts for 7% of the British economy'. (Is that the same as 7% of GDP?)[10] Finally, even if we accept that the financial services sector (however defined) makes an overseas profit of £20 billion a year, we do not know how much of this £20 billion actually returns to the British economy in some form. Since much of the City is now foreign-owned, has been 'Wimbledonised', as Douglas Hurd put it recently, meaning the creation of beautiful conditions for foreign players, manifestly much of it does not.[11]

If we have no real idea how much the City earns, it is no easier to find out how many people the City employs. Anthony Nelson, in the piece quoted already, said that banking and financial services employed over 1.5 million people. A year later the Guardian piece quoted above claimed 2.5 million people in the financial sector. The HMSO publication,Britain 1994: an official

[8] This was still on the Internet in March 1998.

[9] Sunday Telegraph 3 December 1996

[10] Mark Milner, the Guardian 7 March 1998

[11] 'It's Wimbledonisation', Stephen Fay, Independent on Sunday, Section 2, 28 December 1997.

handbook, declared that 'banking, finance and insurance' – a different category – accounted for 12 per cent of employment at the end of 1992. How you would discriminate between these various categories I have no idea, and all of them include many people who are not employed in what most people would recognise as 'the City'. Labour Shadow Minister, Mike O'Brien, in the piece quoted above, claimed that the City employs 2.8 million people – manifestly an absurdity. Mark Milner in 1997 in the Guardian put it at 'something in the region of 600,000'.[12]

THE COSTS OF THE CITY?

Most importantly, the endless stream of articles and press releases about the benefits to the UK of the City/financial sector never mention the costs incurred. What follows is simply a list of areas worth looking at in more detail. There is the price paid by the rest of the economy for the policies which benefit the financial sector. At the top of this list must the incalculable cost of the devastation of the manufacturing sector in the 1980s by the City's high interest/no controls policy implemented by the Thatcher administration.

Then there is the wealth extracted from the rest of the domestic economy by the regime of high interest rates. Between 1970 and 1982 real interest rates never reached 5%. After 1981, after the Tories had scrapped most controls on the financial system, real base interest rates have been less than 5% only once, in 1989, and for much of the period were nearer 8%.[13] Officially, these astronomical real interest rates were 'controlling' inflation; but in fact they are the now familiar edict: lend as much as you like but charge a lot for it. This is a fraud awesome in its simplicity and audacity which makes mafia loan-sharking look amateurish. But how you would calculate its total value, I have no idea.

To this we might add the costs of the great pension rip-off in the late 1980s when two to three million people were persuaded

---

[12] Mark Milner 'The price of Britain's delay' The Guardian, 28 October 28 1997

[13] Figures from Datastream cited in the Independent, 'Your Money' 4 March 1995. The real interest rate is the stated interest rate minus the rate of inflation. These figures are for the minimum rates, the ones charged by the large money lenders at the beginning of the credit system. Interest rates for consumer credit, at the far end of the system for example, are very much higher.

by a government-funded propaganda campaign to leave their occupational pensions and sign up with the private sector's inferior pensions. (Some – but not all – of this will be returned, eventually.) Then there is the costs of the privatisation program. Between 1979 and 1996 the Government received £69 billion from privatisation of assets paid for by taxes: in early the assets sold off were valued at £206 billion.[14] And this does not include the fees charged by the various City institutions for undertaking the privatisation – figures which the Conservative Government refused to reveal on grounds of 'commercial confidentiality'.

There are the costs incurred during the debacle of British membership of the ERM in the late 1980s/90s – further destruction of the domestic economy in another deep recession, billions paid to speculators in the attempt to defend the Sterling-D-mark 2.95 rate, and so forth.

There is the maintenance of Britain's overseas diplomatic, intelligence and military forces to play the supporting cast in the Atlantic alliance which protects the wider, global capitalist system in which the City operates.[15] There is taxes spent on the financial sector. How much has docklands cost since 1979? Your guess is as good as mine: £5 billion? Double that? In 1997 it was reported that the London Docklands Development Corporation had received £1.8 billion since 1981 and 'has swallowed 80% of London's transport budget since 1981, a figure which does not include the new Jubilee Line extension… £2.2b into road and rail

[14] The Observer 8 March 1998. This does not mean that the assets were worth this when they were sold of. See also 'Picking up the tab for the past policy blunders', Larry Elliot and Mark Atkinson, the Guardian 13 March 1998.

[15] There are the less obvious subsidies of the overseas sector - the Export Credits Guarantee scheme, for example, in which the state guarantees companies the money for goods sold abroad, these days increasingly arms sales. 'In the five years to 1984-5, just under 10% of export credits went to defence. In the five years to 1994-5, 30 per cent of export credits went to defence... While exports of pharmaceuticals (excluding chemicals) and medical equipment were $2 billion higher than those for defence in 1994, the unit responsible for promoting these exports within the Department of Health has just four full-time staff. In comparison, Defence Export Services Organisation has some 600 staff.' Cooper p. 139. The Independent reported 27 January 1998 that 'Taxpayers' money has been to underwrite £3 bn in loans to Asian countries whose economies are now collapsing'. More than half of this is arms sales.

links into just one part of the city.'[16] Docklands took 44% of all English Urban Development money spent on road schemes.[17]

Clearly, the domestic financial sector of insurance companies, banks, pension fund management, building societies etc. is a significant sector of the service economy. It is clear also that the City, the 500 plus foreign banks et al, does provide employment in London and the region, both directly and through multiplier effects, chiefly in the service industries. But while I have no idea how a cost-benefit analysis would look if the detailed work was undertaken along the lines suggested above, it seems obvious that the assumption that the City is a 'good thing' for the British economy is highly dubious. And it says much about the dominance of the political and social agenda by the City and the overseas lobby that a cost-benefit analysis of them has never been undertaken.

THE STORY SO FAR.

After being put under central government control during WW2, the City set out to reassert its dominance in the post-war period. The same themes run through the entire period: the desire of the bankers to be allowed to set their own interest rates and continue the City's role as exporters of British capital and manipulators of other peoples' money. Although failing in Operation Robot to 'bounce' the Churchill Government into re-adopting the pre-war system, the use of interest rates to periodically depress the domestic economy to maintain the value of the pound vis-a-vis the dollar was adopted, creating the 'stop-go' economy. This issue ran through into the arrival of the Wilson Government in 1964 and resulted in a series of clashes between Wilson and the overseas lobby which wanted domestic expenditure cut back to defend the value of sterling and maintain the British overseas military/intelligence presence. The City, fronted by Cecil King, began machinating against the Labour Government, and stepped up its funding of the campaign for membership of the EEC.

With the development of the Euro-dollar business centred in London in the late 1960s, the City began to develop as an off-shore financial centre for the world's flight capital and became more

---

[16] Chris Blackhurst Independent on Sunday 28 December 1997.

[17] Guardian 27 June 1995.

powerful. A Conservative Government was returned in 1970 and in the name of 'competition' Edward Heath was conned into enacting the 1952 'Robot' proposals represented as the Competition and Credit Control changes.

As the hysteria about the British Left gathered in the Heath years and took off with the return of Wilson in 1974, the City funded the paramilitary and psy-war outfits of General Sir Walter Walker, David Stirling and George Kennedy Young, the psychological warfare programs of the Freedom Association, and the Thatcher-Joseph faction of the Tory Party.

After the IMF incident, an attempt to persuade the Labour Government to abolish exchange controls in 1977 failed but the Government was persuaded to allow the pound to rise.

In 1979 a City-oriented Conservative Government was returned and, in the name of controlling inflation, reintroduced Competition and Credit Control with the addition of the abolition of exchange controls. British capital began leaving the country and the rise in unemployment predicted by Robot's authors in 1952 duly ensued – as did the asset-stripping of the public sector in the guise of privatisation.

With the North Sea oil revenues to pay for the unemployment; large pay increases for the secret state and the police to encourage them to suppress domestic dissatisfaction – the strong state needed to enforce the so-called free market; tax cuts for the prosperous to purchase cheap privatised assets or invest overseas; and a handy little war in the Falklands to activate the dormant English imperial instincts in the electorate, the Conservatives triumphed in the 1980s.

Finally with the attempt to squeeze the UK economy into the Exchange Rate Mechanism at an over-valued rate for sterling, the destruction of the domestic economy became politically unsustainable. With the third recession since 1979, in 1992 with Britain's forced exit from the ERM, the mass media (and thence the electorate) finally ceased to believe that the Conservatives were the party which knew how to run the economy. But this didn't matter to the overseas lobby which simply switched its support to New Labour which by then was promising essentially the same policies less crudely implemented.

NEW LABOUR, NEW PATRIOTISM?

Addressing Rupert Murdoch's News Corp annual conference in 1995, Tony Blair made the claim that 'The real patriotic case... for those who want Britain to maintain its traditional global role, is for leadership in Europe.'[18] Blair identified the opposition to this as 'outdated and misguided narrow nationalism'. In January 1998 he claimed that an all-party 'patriotic alliance' was forming at Westminster which would back the European project against the 'narrow chauvinism' of the Tory years.[19]

This is one of the key strategies of the Blair faction: adopt the language and symbols of patriotism – wave the flag, parade the British bulldog, as Labour did in the election campaign – but define being patriotic not as concern for or pride in the country (patris = Greek for fatherland) but as support for Britain's world role, activating the circuits of nostalgia for Empire which are hard-wired into the British, and particularly the English, psyche. Part of the Conservative Party's electoral appeal in the 1980s under Mrs Thatcher was her appeal to British – sometimes – and particularly, English nationalism. But just like his mentor, Mrs Thatcher, Tony Blair is adopting the language of patriotism as cover for the interests of the overseas lobby.

For the Blair 'project', patriotism-as-internationalism has the added bonus of making opposition by the Labour Left extremely difficult. With the Blair definition of patriotism as supporting Britain's overseas economy – he said 'global role' but it is the investments which matter; without them there would be no overseas role – to argue for the interests of the domestic economy entails arguing against the interests of the overseas economy; and, within the Blairite framework this creates the bizarre situation in which the Labour Left is in danger of accused of being chauvinistic, nationalist and not patriotic! And if the British Left is deeply uncomfortable with the language of patriotism,[20] opposing Blair's patriotism-as-internationalism is to risk contamination by nationalism, which is absolute anathema to them.

---

[18] The Times 17 July 1995

[19] 'Blair warns of euro "shock"', the Guardian 21 January 1998

[20] In her first volume of memoirs, The Path to Power (p. 43) Mrs Thatcher described Tony Benn as 'an English patriot'. I suspect this is not how Tony Benn sees himself!

CONTAMINATION

Political contamination is one the key concepts in understanding British politics.[21] Given the dominant right-left structure of politics which, despite New Labour's attempts to fudge it, we still have in this country people on the centre-left of the spectrum who are concerned not to be associated with certain ideas or people on the right. This process obviously works in reverse, people on the right do not wish to be seen to be associated with people or ideas on the left. To be associated with an idea from, or people belonging to, the ideological opposite is to risk contamination; and with the collapse of the Soviet empire the most potent contamination concept in British mainstream politics today is no longer communism but nationalism.

Nationalism contaminates the British Left because of its association with racism, fascism and anti-semitism. Or rather, nationalism contaminates on the English Left because of nationalism's association with the English far Right and thus with racism, fascism, and anti-semitism. For in Wales and Scotland and Ireland[22] it is possible – and intellectually respectable – to be a left nationalist and not really risk contamination by the far right. In Scotland, Wales and even Northern Ireland, the National Front, the British National Party et al have singularly failed to make even the tiny in-roads they have in England because in the non-English parts of the United Kingdom nationalism is regarded as legitimate and is embraced by mainstream political parties.

Opposing the European Union (EU), a section of the British Labour Left is in danger of contamination by a section of the Tory Right, which also opposes the EU. Labour Left opponents of the EU thus to have to try to ensure that they are not contaminated by such an association, that they are not perceived as nationalists – 'little Englanders' – with its xenophobic and racist overtones. Tony Benn commented that, in the debate about the

[21] I was introduced to the notion of political contamination by Mike Peters. In a footnote to his essay on the Bilderberg group in Lobster 32, Peters noted that the US Left had lost interest in the study of the power elite because the subject had become 'contaminated' by the interest in it taken by the US Right. Political contamination (PC) is a consequence of not being Political Correct (PC)!

[22] Northern Ireland, divided as it is, contains two identities; or three if you count the Ulster Protestant and British as distinct. The Northern Irish, former National Front member, David Kerr, publishes a magazine there called Ulster Nation.

European Union:

'Anyone who doubts the wisdom of accepting an unelected central bank is called [by TV journalists] a nationalist or a trouble-maker, or is assumed to be launching a crude leadership bid.'[23] Here is Bill Morris, General Secretary of the Transport and General Workers, preparing to oppose a single European currency:

'I do not approach this issue from a nationalist position. The flag-waving, tub-thumping tabloid chauvinism of the Tory right is alien to the traditions of the trade union movement.'[24]

Here is 'left-wing Eurosceptic' Walter Cairns welcoming the election defeat of Michael Portillo:

'Had he won, his chances of his obtaining the leadership of the Tory party on an anti-European ticket would have been extremely high. This would have mean that the Eurosceptic cause would have been even more solidly entrenched into the far-right camp – thus smearing by association those who have severe reservations about the EU for reasons other than blind xenophobia.'[25]

And here is Diane Abbot MP, from the Labour Left, in The Observer (Business) on 18 August 1996, underneath a piece by John Redwood, from the Tory Right, both of them opposing European Monetary Union:

'The debate on economic and monetary union has been hijacked by the Tory Party right wing. But there is also a socialist case against it. And it has nothing to do with the backward-looking nationalism of the Tory little Englanders. On the contrary, for true internationalists...'[26]

Nationalism contaminates because the Labour Left, and the whole of the British Left, sees itself as internationalist. Nationalism is regarded as one of the sources of all evil in the

---

[23] The Guardian 18 March 1997

[24] The Guardian 9 September 1996

[25] The Guardian (letters) 3 May 1997 It is sadly typical of the Labour Left that Cairns thinks - or professes to think - that right-wing hostility to the European Union is simply motivated by xenophobia.

[26] The claim that the right has 'hi-jacked' the issue is nonsense. There has always been a section of the Tory Right which, like the Labour Left, opposed the EEC and the European Union. I have no idea what Abbott's 'true internationalism' means.

world: vide World Wars 1 and 2, vide Yugoslavia, etc, etc. But the British Left's hostility to nationalism is flexible. When the British Left helped in the struggle to free the British colonies it was working with nationalists. The Left supports Irish nationalism and supported Vietnamese and South African nationalism.

These nationalists did not contaminate the British Left, for the left perceives nationalism as legitimate when it is opposing a colonial oppressor, when it can be called national self-determination. Here is the basis of the legitimacy of Welsh, Scots and Irish nationalism: their oppressor is England. At any rate, the British Left does not assume that qua nationalists, the Scots and Welsh Nats are racists and fascists; and never has, as far as I am aware. But this Welsh and Scottish nationalism is not even basically anti-English. Scots and Welsh Nationalists don't see the people in the North (or Midlands, or East or West) of England as their oppressor. Their oppressor is in London and the Home Counties – the English Establishment as it used to be known, which at its core is the City of London and the overseas lobby.

This is the nexus of interests which has been perceived, intermittently, by sections of the domestic British economy, from the days of the Tariff Reform League before World War 1 through to Neil Kinnock and his economics adviser John Eatwell, circa 1984/5, as the enemy of the interests of the rest of Britain. It is ironic that it should be a Welshman, Neil Kinnock, and the Scot, John Smith, who led the Labour Party away from its historical role representing the non-metropolitan areas of England, with those of Wales and Scotland, towards its current role as stooges for the overseas lobby in general and the City of London in particular.

At the heart of the New Labour project, as Blair's speeches make clear, is acceptance of EU membership within the new deregulated global market dominated by the trans-national corporations and the foreign exchange dealers. There are New Labour supporters who have persuaded themselves that this represents a really big step forward. The political journalist at the Observer, Andrew Adonis, announced in the issue of 15 March 1998 that he was leaving the paper to join the government as an adviser. He wrote in his valedictory column:

'George Orwell famously described England as a Victorian

family with the wrong members in charge. This is the social democratic moment for my generation. If it succeeds we remove the family from the anti-European neo-liberals who took over in the late Thatcher years, after 40 years – following the first phase of Attlee's reforms – of lacklustre leadership by Left and Right alike.'

Mr Adonis, like other idealistic EU enthusiasts, has misread the situation.[27] He ought to go back and read the section of Blair's speech to the Murdoch gathering which begins, 'We asked the Americans...' Labour is now pro-EU only in the sense of continuing the traditional US policy of using the UK as insurance against the European Union becoming 'protectionist' – i.e. setting up trade barriers to non-EU goods and capital. The maintenance of global free trade, that is freedom for US capital, remains the predominant US policy objective. The British overseas lobby wants the same thing. This is why the Franco-German core of the EU has always been suspicious of Britain's role in the EEC/EU. While the British Foreign Office appears enthusiastic about the EU, it is the same British Foreign Office which is working most enthusiastically for EU expansion in the hope that it will frustrate the central French-German bloc's drive towards federalism – and the possibility of resistance to US capital.

New Labour wants a free market European Union – with a single currency if it must. The 1997 Labour election manifesto on Europe stated:

'Our vision of Europe is an alliance of independent nations choosing to co-operate to achieve the goals they cannot achieve alone. We oppose a European federal superstate.' This is exactly the Thatcher line and explains in large part why Mrs Thatcher has expressed such approval for Blair and called him 'a patriot' after one of their meetings after Labour's 1997 election victory.'

---

[27] Mr Adonis, metropolitan slip showing, writes of England when he presumably really means Britain.

Chapter Ten

TORY LITE

After the capture of the Labour leadership by the Blair faction, Labour was supported by the overseas lobby – most of the major media, multinational capital, the Foreign Office, the City – because the Blairites seemed to have the Labour Party under better control than John Major did the Tories, while pursuing essentially the same overseas lobby-friendly policies. The joke about the New Labour being Tory Lite was spot-on. It was, as I noted earlier, the final triumph of the overseas lobby: the one major party which, however incoherently and ineptly, had opposed it, had been neutralised.

A number of factors led to this. One was the failure to create anything resembling a domestic economy lobby in this country. The Confederation of British Industry, the nearest this country has had to such a lobby in the past 30 years, represents all sectors of the economy, the interests of several of which are in opposition, (exporters versus importers, most obviously), and is thus ineffective against the overseas lobby's control of the agenda.[1]

Assisted by MI5's allowing the CPGB to operate within the labour movement, fantasies of socialism survived within the Labour Party. This prevented much of the labour movement from perceiving that its important allies were to be found within the managers of the domestic economy. Among Labour Party members and within the wider labour movement the left/right dichotomy created a value system in which to be left was good, more left better, most left best; and the corollary, right bad, more right worse, most right worst. Critically, in this value system the concepts of nation, national interest and patriotism, had all been

[1] See Grant and Marsh.

assigned to the right and were therefore anathema, sources of contamination to the left.[2] As a result, the argument that the EEC/EU was a 'capitalist club' lost its force when the Labour Party and labour movement collectively gave up on socialism in the 1980s, and they found it increasingly difficult to resist the appeal of the EEC. With socialism gone, the only ground left on which to oppose the EEC was that it was not in our national interest to be members of the EEC/EU: and this option was effectively precluded by its adoption by a section of the Tory Right. Only a handful of Labour MPs outside the socialist minority groupings (chiefly the Campaign Group), notably Peter Shore, Austin Mitchell and Bryan Gould (before his departure in despair for New Zealand) were willing to stand publicly against the EEC tide and risk contamination by the right, and ridicule by the major media, most of which had long been persuaded to ignore the real issues and costs of EEC/EU membership and had consigned the anti-EEC/EU groups to the fatal category of cranks, standing in the way of History and Destiny.[3]

The basic facts on the UK's EU membership are stark. At today's prices since Britain joined in 1972 the UK taxpayer has paid a total of £47 billion for the privilege of being a member of the EEC/EC/EU.[4] To which we might add the cost of loss of fishing rights, surrendered to the EEC as part of the price Heath (secretly) paid in 1972; the destruction of a considerable chunk of the British countryside under the impact of EEC agricultural subsidies; and the costs of the recession caused by membership of the ERM in 1990-92.

---

[2] Tom Nairn could lampoon the Labour Party of the 1970s in his brilliant polemic The Left Against Europe (Penguin 1973) as national-socialist: but while its members and leaders would have divided on the socialist half of the term, almost none of them would have accepted the nationalist half.

[3] And no, I'm not exaggerating: some EU-enthusiasts really do think in these terms. See, for example, Ian Black's piece in the Guardian 5 December 1997, titled 'View from platform 24'. Its subheading warned us that 'the train of destiny is about to leave without us'.

[4] Labour Euro-safeguards Campaign Bulletin November 1997. Lest you consider the source biased - which it is - the House of Commons Library published a Research Paper (No 97/137, December 1997), EC Finance, which showed (p. 37) that the UK average net contributions to the EC/EU for the 1992-96 period was £2,734,000 - nearly £14 billion in those five years alone.

This extraordinary destruction – and the price paid for it – has been possible because in all the negotiations with the EEC/EU it has been the interests of the overseas lobby which predominated; and the overseas lobby, and their representatives in the Foreign Office, were entirely happy to surrender sections of the British domestic economy as bargaining chips in the process. The power of that lobby is illustrated by the fact that while the Treasury opposed EEC entry, it was simply ignored. Lord Croham, then Permanent Secretary at the Treasury, commented recently in a symposium on the Heath years:

'In the 1960s the Treasury was less enthusiastic about membership of the European Community than Heath. This lack of enthusiasm was carried through into the 1970s. The Treasury was also quite pessimistic about the country's balance of payments outlook and the negative balance of payments effects which would be produced upon joining the Common Market.'[5]

Labour's macro-economic policies are essentially those of its Conservative predecessors. Afraid to challenge the overseas lobby, Labour is committed to the free movement of capital, carrying on the UK economy's traditional, imperial-originated bias towards overseas investment. In 1979 Barbara Castle MP, who had been in the Labour Government until 1976, noted that while British direct overseas investment – i.e. plant, machinery etc. – between 1966-76 had increased by 579%, manufacturing investment in the UK had increased by only 17.6% in the same period.[6]

Between 1978 and 1995 outward investment from Britain was £137.8 billion (between 1992 and 1996 alone, £97.9 billion).[7] This would have been politically unsustainable were it not the fact that the mid-1980s, as UK capital poured out of Britain with the abolition of exchange controls in 1980, the Conservatives discovered that while their policies of recession and smashing the trade unions were not persuading domestic capital to invest much in

[5] Kandiah (ed.) p. 196. See also Reid p. 72. 'Cabinet Office "keepers" were sent to accompany Treasury officials on some missions in case they handled things in discussions in Europe in ways that were not in line with Heath's approach.' Ball and Seldon p. 84

[6] Krammick (ed.) pp. 46 and 48

[7] Sunday Telegraph 18 August 1996 and 22 March 1998. Looking at another period, 'Since 1979 inward investment has leapt from £22 bn to £140 bn.' Bill Jamieson, Sunday Telegraph 21 January 1996

Britain, foreign capital, especially US and Far Eastern capital, began to see low-wage, depressed, non-regulated Britain as an ideal door into the EEC. Between 1978 and 1995 inward investment into the UK was £93.5 billion.[8] (Looking at a slightly different period, 1992 -1996, the inward total was £53.2 billion.[9]) These substantial sums do not conceal that fact that between 1978-95 the UK economy experienced a net loss of £44.3 billion – roughly equivalent to the amount paid to the EU for the UK's membership in the same period – another part of the price we pay for the overseas lobby.

To outgoing UK investment, a strong pound allows UK capital to purchase foreign assets relatively cheaply. To incoming investment the UK offers low corporation taxes and personal taxes,[10] 'flexible' (i.e. docile, frightened, increasingly non-unionised, instantly disposable) labour, tax breaks for investment, relatively few regulations, access to rest of the European Union, the use of English and a generally civilised society for managers to live in (lots of golf courses and private schools – the things that seem to matter to prospective managers).

Of that inward investment 41% is from the US; and 34% of the total UK overseas assets are in the US. This is the basis of the renewed Anglo-American 'special relationship' today. The British domestic economy may be too feeble these days to provide the armed forces the overseas lobby might like, but the UK still has a seat at the UN's top table and can still play the role of 'international support' for US policies, no matter how obnoxious or self-defeating.

To sustain this system of open markets, free movement of capital out of the UK, the flow of inwards investment has to be maintained; and this can only happen as long as the UK maintains its competitive edge by being less regulated, paying lower wages, and charging firms lower taxes. Tony Blair may lecture other EU

[8] Hansard vol. 248, col. 164, cited in the the Guardian (Weekend) 11March 1965

[9] Sunday Telegraph 22 March 1998. The reader may notice that there are some discrepancies between these various figures, but they are relatively slight and all such official figures are subject to periodic revision. If the figures are wrong it won't be by much.

[10] A spokesman for the Invest in Britain Bureau said, after Gordon Brown's March 1998 budget, 'The cut in corporation tax to 30% puts our company tax rate among the lowest in the world.' Sunday Telegraph, 22 March 1998, B7.

countries on the necessity of their copying the British model – the one Mrs Thatcher stumbled upon – but that they actually do so is the last thing the British state's economic planners want. Were EU countries to copy the UK model, the major reason overseas investment comes to the UK rather than to other EU members would vanish. The logic of the new world order, the embrace of which is what counts as 'modernisation' for the Blair faction, is of countries competing with each other for multinational capital by offering more profit: in other words, lower wages, lower taxes and more subsidies. In this 'race to the bottom' for the favours of multinational corporations, chiefly thanks to Mrs Thatcher, Britain has a head start on its current EU competitors.

Britain is in the most precarious position. Its industry has been run down; it is increasingly dependent upon footloose foreign capital for productive domestic investment. The agricultural sector is being run down, even though we produce less than half our food and a tiny fraction of our timber. Coal mining is almost gone (but we are importing coal); the fishing industry is being run-down (along with with the fish-stocks of the North Sea).

Most of the revenues of the North Sea have either been dissipated in paying for the unemployment of the Thatcher years or exported abroad to benefit the productive economies of other countries (and UK shareholders and those in the UK whose pension funds are invested overseas). The British merchant fleet is almost non-existent. (Another Falklands War couldn't be fought

---

[14] The Observer 8 March 1998. This does not mean that the assets were worth this when they were sold of. See also 'Picking up the tab for the past policy blunders', Larry Elliot and Mark Atkinson, the Guardian 13 March 1998.

[15] There are the less obvious subsidies of the overseas sector - the Export Credits Guarantee scheme, for example, in which the state guarantees companies the money for goods sold abroad, these days increasingly arms sales. 'In the five years to 1984-5, just under 10% of export credits went to defence. In the five years to 1994-5, 30 per cent of export credits went to defence... While exports of pharmaceuticals (excluding chemicals) and medical equipment were $2 billion higher than those for defence in 1994, the unit responsible for promoting these exports within the Department of Health has just four full-time staff. In comparison, Defence Export Services Organisation has some 600 staff.' Cooper p. 139. The Independent reported 27 January 1998 that 'Taxpayers' money has been to underwrite £3 bn in loans to Asian countries whose economies are now collapsing'. More than half of this is arms sales.

because there are no longer enough British-flagged ships of the right kind to commandeer and mount such an expedition.) Britain has never been more vulnerable in peace-time.

As the British domestic economy shrinks the choices open to the government shrink. As manufacturing declines the one bit which the government encourages, military hardware, which helps maintain its overseas role, grows as a proportion of it. As the coal industry shrinks our dependence on the nuclear industry grows and we will continue to be the dustbin for the world's nuclear waste. As we become more and more an economy dependent on the whims of tourism, environmentally disastrous projects like the expansion of Heathrow and Manchester airports, become unstoppable. An 'ethical foreign policy'? Not if jobs are at stake.[11]

Mrs Thatcher famously said that there was no such thing as society, just individuals and families. As so often, she got it wrong. The exact opposite is true. In fact that there is nothing but society; individuals and families exist within and in relation to society. The so-called 'private sector' is dependent upon, is all too frequently parasitic upon, society – and the public sector. The private medical sector is parasitic on the NHS: it does not train doctors, nurses or technicians; does not develop new drugs and techniques; provides no emergency services. The private education sector is parasitic upon the state sector: it trains no teachers, funds no higher or further education, develops no curricula.

The entire infrastructure of society from transport to schools via the armed forces, legal and justice system, health service – the infrastructure which makes 'the free market' possible, which facilitates capital formation, is provided by the public sector. Or if you like, by the state – by the taxes of the many. It is on this basis that the state used to believe it had the right to intervene in the free movement of capital and try to prevent the wealth created in Britain leaving the country and direct some of it into socially useful rather than merely profitable areas. In economic terms, the

[11] I have written book reviews for Tribune since 1986. The first review of mine which did not appear was of a book attacking Britain's military-industrial complex, Neil Cooper's The Business of Death (I.B. Tauris, 1997). A couple of months before I submitted my review the unions represented in the British arms industry had run a full-page ad in Tribune saying, basically, 'jobs are at stake'. These two events are, of course, not connected.

other concept of patriotism, the one which is concerned with what happens here, the one rejected by the Blair faction, starts with the idea that wealth generated in the UK, by UK resources, should stay here, and should be forced to do so, if necessary.[12]

As the pound was pushed above 3 Dm in early 1998 by the series of interest rate rises which followed Labour 'setting free' the Bank of England, Ken Livingstone said,

'You've got to defend your own industry and create jobs for your own people first. You can't just allow market forces to wipe them out.'[13]

Livingstone's 'your own people', like those other mealy-mouthed expressions which trip off the tongues of Labour Party politicians, 'our people' and 'all our people', is the closest the Labour Left feels able to move towards the language of nation and national interest without feeling threatened by the contamination of nationalism. But where else is the Labour Left to go but back to the nationalist half of the national-socialist tandem which Tom Nairn, in the full pomp of Marxist triumphalism, found so absurd in the 1973? The alternatives are either vacuous: 'true internationalism', whatever that means; or absurd: 'a socialist European Union', which is about as distant a prospect as the proletarian revolution advocated by the Trotskyite splinters.

The Labour Party is usually running years behind events. It reaffirmed its commitment to UK nuclear weapons just at the point when not only was the cost of the Trident programme making deep inroads into conventional forces, and was opposed by most the the armed forces not directly involved in it, the Soviet empire, against whose 'threat' it was supposed to protect us, began to collapse.

It become Euro-enthusiasts just when the preposterous, centralising, neo-Stalinist ambitions of the EU were finally being revealed.

[12] In the case of wealth generated in the UK by non-UK resources, for example, by inward investment, there is no such case.

[13] Guardian 16 March 1998. Since the EU prohibits defence of 'your own industry' except in extreme cases, quite how Ken squares this with his support for British membership for the EU and a single currency, I don't know. In practice most EU countries cheat when they have to. The British state, with a long tradition of instinctive and institutional support for market forces, appears to cheat least of all - ensuring that we get the worst of all possible worlds.

It became free market enthusiasts just when the damage the free market was causing became clear to all but the most fervent ideologues on the libertarian right who could fend it off reality with talk of jam tomorrow.

It became privatisation enthusiasts just when the damage privatisation had caused had become clear and the electorate, ripped-off by the most of the privatised utility companies, was turning against privatisation.

It has become workfare enthusiasts just when the evidence of its failure has begun to appear in countries – New Zealand, Canada, USA – which have tried it.

In short, Labour – at any rate the Blair faction which took over the party – became Thatcherites just when the disastrous effects of those years were finally becoming unavoidable.

Changing Labour Party policy takes a long time. The analogy of the super-tanker changing course is apt. It takes a long time to change course, even if you can get a message to the bridge; and in the Labour Party there are always a large number of people on the bridge who have committed themselves to the wrong course; who are reluctant in the extreme to admit they made a mistake; who care less about the right course than they do about being seen to have made a mistake; and who are guarded by people whose job it is to make sure no course-changing messages get through. But change course it will have to do.

---

[18] The Times 17 July 1995

[19] 'Blair warns of euro "shock"', the Guardian 21 January 1998

[20] In her first volume of memoirs, The Path to Power (p. 43) Mrs Thatcher described Tony Benn as 'an English patriot'. I suspect this is not how Tony Benn sees himself!

Bibliography

All books have been published in
London unless otherwise stated

Agee, Philip and Wolf, Louis (eds.)
Dirty Work: the CIA in Western Europe, Zed Books, 1978.
Anderson, Paul and Mann, Nyta
Safety First: the Making of New Labour, Granta Books, 1997
Ball, Stuart and Seldon, Anthony
The Heath Government 1970-74, Longman, 1996
Barker, Terry & Brailovsky, V (eds.)
Oil or Industry , Academic Press, 1981
Benn, Tony
Against the Tide: Diaries 1973-76, Hutchinson, 1980
Office Without Power, Diaries 1968-72, Arrow, 1988
Blair, Tony New Britain, Fourth Estate, 1996
Bloch, Jonathan & Fitzgerald, Patrick
British Intelligence and Covert Action, Junction, 1983
Block, Fred. L.
The Origins of International Economic Disorder, University of California Press, 1977
Blum, William
The CIA: a forgotten history, Zed Books, 1986
Bower, Tom
The Perfect English Spy, Heinemann, 1995
Boyson, Rhodes
Centre Forward: A Radical Conservative Programme, Temple Smith, 1978
Bradley, Ian
Breaking the Mould? The Birth and Prospects of the Social Democratic Party, Martin Robertson, Oxford, 1981
Brittan, Samuel
Steering the Economy Penguin, Harmondsworth, 1971
Broad, Roger and Geiger, Tim
The 1975 British Referendum on Europe: a Witness Seminar' in

Contemporary Record Vol. 10, no. 3, 1996
Bruce-Gardyne, Jock
Whatever happened to the Quiet Revolution? Charles Knight and Co., 1974
Burk, Kathleen, and Cairncross, Alec
Goodbye Great Britain: the 1976 IMF Crisis, Yale University Press, 1992
Butler, David and Kavanagh, Dennis
The British General Election of October 1974, Macmillan, 1975
Callaghan, James
Time and Chance, Collins, 1987
Campbell, John
Edward Heath, Cape, 1993.
Carew, Anthony Labour Under the Marshall Plan, Manchester University Press, Manchester, 1987
Cassin, Youssef (ed.)
Finance and Financiers in European History , Cambridge University Press, Cambridge, 1992
Castle, Barbara
The Castle Diaries 1974-76, Book Club Associates, 1980
Coates, Ken (ed.)
What Went Wrong?, Spokesman, Nottingham, 1979
Cockett, Richard
Thinking The Unthinkable: Think-tanks and the Economic Counter-Revolution 1931-1983, Harper Collins, 1985
Cole, John
As It Seemed to Me, Weidenfeld and Nicolson, 1995
Coleman, Peter
The Liberal Conspiracy, Collier Macmillan, 1989
Cooper, Neil
The Business of Death: Britain's Arms Trade at Home and Abroad, I.B. Tauris, 1997
Crozier, Brian
Free Agent, HarperCollins, 1993
Crouch, Colin (ed.)
State and Economy in Contemporary Capitalism, Croom Helm, 1979
Curtis, Mark
The Ambiguities of Power, Zed Books, 1995
Desai, Radhika
Intellectuals and Socialism: 'Social Democrats' and the Labour Party, Lawrence and Wishart, 1994
Dorril, Stephen and Ramsay, Robin

Smear! Wilson and the Secret State, Fourth Estate, 1991
Donoughue, Bernard
Prime Minister: the Conduct of Policy under Harold Wilson and James Callaghan, Jonathan Cape, 1987
DuCann, Edward
Two lives, Images Publishing, Upton on Severn, 1995
Eringer, Robert
The Global Manipulators, Pentacle Books, Bristol (UK) 1980
Fay, Stephen and Young, Hugo
The Day the £ Nearly Died, Sunday Times (pamphlet), 1978
Finer, S.E.
Anonymous Empire: A Study of the Lobby in Great Britain, Pall Mall, 1969
Forte, Charles
Forte: the Autobiography of Charles Forte, Sidgwick and Jackson, 1986
Frazier, Howard (ed.)
Uncloaking the CIA, The Free Press/Macmillan, New York, 1978
Geddes, Andrew
'Labour and the European Community 1973-93', in Contemporary Record, Vol. 8, No. 2, Autumn 1994
Gordon, Charles
The Cedar Story, Sinclair-Stevenson, 1993
Gorman, Teresa
The Bastards, Pan, 1993
Gould, Bryan
Goodbye To All That, Macmillan, 1995
Grant, Wyn (ed.)
Business and Politics in Britain (2nd edition), Macmillan, 1993
Grant, Wyn and Marsh, David
The CBI, Hodder and Stoughton, 1977
Green, Ewan
'The Influence of the City Over British Economic Policy', in Cassin (ed.)
Haines, Joe
The Politics of Power, Jonathan Cape, 1977
Halcrow, Morrison
Keith Joseph: A Single Mind, Macmillan, 1989.
Haseler, Stephen
The Battle for Britain, Leo Cooper, 1994
The Gaitskellites, Macmillan, 1969
Healey, Denis
The Time of My Life, Michael Joseph, 1989

Heller, Robert and Willatt, Norris
Can You Trust Your Bank?, Weidenfeld and Nicolson, 1977
Hennessy, Peter
Muddling Through, Gollancz, 1996
Whitehall, Secker and Warburg, 1989
Hirsch, Fred and Fletcher, Richard
The CIA and the Labour Movement, Spokesman, Nottingham, 1977
Hughes, Colin and Wintour, Patrick
Labour Rebuilt, Fourth Estate, 1990
Institute for Historical Research
Witness Seminar Transcript: The Launch of the SDP 1979-83, London 1991
Witness Seminar Transcript: The Campaign for Democratic Socialism, London, 1990
Jay, Douglas
Sterling: a plea for moderation, Sidgwick and Jackson, 1985
Jenkins, Roy
A Life at the Centre, Macmillan, 1991
Johnson, Christopher
The Economy Under Mrs Thatcher 1979 90, Penguin, Harmondsworth, 1991.
Kaiser, Philip
Journeying Far and Wide, Maxwell Macmillan International, Oxford, 1992
Kandiah, Michael David (ed.)
'The Heath Government: a Witness Seminar' in Contemporary Record, Vol. 9, No. 1, 1995
Keegan, William
Mrs Thatcher's Economic Experiment, Penguin, Harmondsworth, 1985
Mr Lawson's Gamble, Hodder and Stoughton, 1989
King, Cecil,
The Cecil King Diary 1970-74, Cape, 1975
Kisch, Richard
The Private Life of Public Relations, MacGibbon and Kee, 1964
Krammick, Isaac (ed.)
Is Britain Dying?, Cornell University, USA, 1979
Kwitney, Jonathan
Endless Enemies, Congdon and Weed, New York, 1984
Lawson, Nigel
The View From No. 11, Corgi, 1992
Lewis, Julian

Changing Direction: British Military Planning for Post-war Strategic Defense, The Sherwood Press, 1988
Llewelyn, David T. (ed.)
The Framework of UK Monetary Policy, Heinemann, 1982
Macdougall, Donald
Don and Mandarin: Memoirs of an Economist, John Murray, 1987
McSmith, Andy
John Smith, Playing the Long Game, Verso, 1993
Michie, Alistair and Hoggart, Simon
The Pact, Quartet, 1978
Minkin, Lewis
The Contentious Alliance, University of Edinburgh Press, Edinburgh, 1991
Moran, Michael
The Politics of Banking, MacMillan, 1986
'Finance Capital and Pressure Group Politics in Britain', in The British Journal of Political Science, Vol. 11, 1981
Nairn, Tom
The Break-up of Britain, Verso, 1981
Neil, Andrew Full Disclosure, Macmillan, 1996
Newton, Scott
'Operation "Robot" and the Political Economy of Sterling Convertibility', European University Institute Working Paper, no. 86/256, Italy, 1986
The Profits of Peace, Clarendon, Oxford, 1996
Newton, Scott and Porter, Dilwyn
Modernization Frustrated: the Politics of Industrial Decline in Britain since 1900, Unwin Hyman, 1988
The New York Times
The Watergate Hearings, Bantam Books, New York, 1973
Norton-Taylor, Richard, Lloyd, Mark and Cook, Stephen
Knee Deep In Dishonour: the Scott Report and its Aftermath, Gollancz, 1996
Owen, David
Time to Declare , Penguin, Harmondsworth, 1992
Parkinson, Cecil
Right At the Centre, Weidenfeld and Nicolson, 1992
Pliatzky, Leo
Getting and Spending, Basil Blackwell, Oxford, 1982.
Pliatzky, Leo
The Treasury Under Mrs Thatcher, Basil Blackwell, Oxford, 1989
Ramsay, Robin
The Clandestine Caucus, a Lobster special issue, Hull, 1996

Ranelagh, John
Thatcher's People, Fontana, 1991
Reid, Margaret
The Secondary Banking Crisis 1973-5, Macmillan, 1982
Richter, Irving
Political Purpose in Trade Unions, Allen and Unwin, 1973
Riddell, Peter
The Thatcher Government, Martin Robertson, 1983
Ridley, Nicholas
My Style of Government, Hutchinson, 1991
Rintoul, John
Tony Blair, Little Brown, 1995
Roberts, Ernie
Strike Back, (self published) Orpington, Kent, 1994
Roseveare, Henry
The Treasury , Allen and Unwin, 1966
Salter, Arthur
Slave of the Lamp, Weidenfeld and Nicolson, 1967
Seldon, Anthony and Ball, Stuart (eds.)
Conservative Century: the Conservative Party since 1900, Oxford University Press, 1994
Shaw, Eric
Discipline and Discord in the Labour Party, Manchester University Press, Manchester, 1988.
Shoup, Laurence H. and Minter, William
Imperial Brain Trust, Monthly Review Press, London and New York, 1977
Smith, David
The Rise and Fall of Monetarism, Penguin, Harmondsworth, 1987.
Smith, Raymond and Zametica, John
'The Cold Warrior: Clement Attlee reconsidered, 1945-7 in International Affairs, Spring 1985
Smith, Richard Harris
OSS: the Secret History of America's First Central Intelligence Agency, University of California Press, Berkeley, 1972
Stephens, Philip
Politics and the Pound, Macmillan, 1996
Strange, Susan
Sterling and British Policy, Oxford University Press, 1971
Teague, Paul
'The TUC and the European Community' in Millenium: Journal of International Studies, Vol. 18, No.1

Tebbitt, Norman
Upwardly Mobile (2nd edition), Futura, 1989
Thatcher, Margaret
The Downing Street Years, HarperCollins, 1993.
The Path to Power, HarperCollins, 1995
Thomas, Hugh (ed.)
Crisis in the Civil Service, Anthony Blond, 1968
Wapshott, Nicholas and Brock, George
Thatcher, Macdonald, 1983
Weiler, Peter
British Labour and the Cold War, Stanford University Press, Standford, California, 1988
Whitehead, Phillip
The Writing on the Wall: Britain in the Seventies, Michael Joseph, 1985
Wigham, Eric
What's Wrong With The Unions?, Penguin, Harmondsworth, 1961
Williams, Philip M. (ed.)
The Diary of Hugh Gaitskell 1945-56, Jonathan Cape, 1983
Wilson, Harold
The Labour Government 1964-70 , Weidenfeld and Nicolson and Michael Joseph, 1971
Final Term: The Labour Government 1974-76 Weidenfeld and Nicolson, 1979
Windlesham, Lord
Communication and Political Power, Cape, 1966
Wright, Peter and Greengrass, Paul
Spycatcher, Viking, New York, 1987

Prawn Cocktail Party

An extract from LAWYERS ON THE SPOT

by Donna Leigh-Kile

...Top judges in Britain have become third-age rebels. They outmanoeuvred and outflanked the former Tory government in the past two years with skills a matador would envy - notwithstanding their average age of 60. Whether they maintain this role under the Labour government is the subject of riveting speculation amongst the legal profession.

The time-worn, vicious swipe that judges dwell in ivory towers loses its sting when one considers that they opposed the Conservatives, who were forced to compromise on the down-to-earth issues of minimum sentences, asylum seekers and police bugging. Due to extremely unusual and outspoken criticism on policy from the massed ranks of the judiciary, the minimum sentences bill was modified, allowing judges to impose a lesser sentence 'in the interests of justice'; senior judges ruled that it was illegal for the government to withdraw benefits from asylum seekers whose applications to stay in the UK had not yet been determined; and they won a change in the police 'bugging' bill stipulating that authorisation must be obtained from a judge, not just a chief constable, when the police want to tap 'phones.

There has also been an explosion of judicial review cases, overturning all sorts of decisions made by central and local government and financial regulatory bodies in the last few years, making it one of the most fashionable areas of law in which to practise. "Indeed, the way the judiciary has taken on the government makes the Bar appear reactionary in comparison," says radical barrister Quincy Whitaker. Another barrister says that the judges' independent stance in the 1990's follows decades of toeing the government line, particularly in the late1960's and 1970's, which coincided with a number of grave miscarriages of justice, some of which are only now coming to light.

Despite praise for the judiciary's current collective show of strength from those within the legal profession, many lawyers, clients and the public view some individual judges as proof of the principle that people rise to the limits of their capacities, and then a bit more. No lawyer questioned for this book could explain why otherwise some good, even excellent, lawyers undergo a complete personality change or become incompetent when they take to the Bench. It is called 'judge-itis.'

"I do wonder what happens to these very sensible barristers who go mad when they get on the High Bench," says a long-time barrister's clerk. "Whether it's the power, I don't know, but they suddenly change for the worse. The opinions you know they held at the Bar are sometimes completely at odds with the decisions they are making as judges.

"I said to one barrister whom I've known for twenty years and who was about to become a judge: 'Don't get like some of the others.' He told me to keep calling him 'Andrew'. There are some who insist that you call them Mr. Justice So-and-So, even when you have been on first-name terms with them for years and years."

Bouts of overweening self-regard on the bench, or ignorance of sex practices and pop stars, resulting in judges being ridiculed by the press, disguise far deeper concerns. Partisan judges, who violate the basic tenet that justice should be done and be seen to be done, are the bane of lawyers' lives and have, in their view, seriously damaged the public's faith in the legal system.

Dick Ferguson, QC, was involved in the penultimate appeal of the 'Birmingham Six', at which Lord Chief Justice Lane uttered the famous words: "The longer this hearing has gone on the more convinced this court has become that the verdict of the jury (in the original trial) was correct."

Ferguson says: "What happened in those 'miscarriage-of-justice' cases, and there were a number of them, not all Irish, was that the establishment, as represented by the top echelons of the legal profession, refused to countenance the possibility of error by the lower courts. Instead of approaching the appeals with an open mind, they approached them determined to uphold the convictions.

"Even when the evidence had reached a stage where it should have been obvious to them that it was time to admit failure, they still tried to cling to the convictions. And it was only when the convictions were finally wrested from them that they gave up. Of course, that much publicised delay has done irreparable damage to the image of our legal system."

Bias is no less invidious at county court level. Barrister Jacqueline Perry recalls representing a man seeking custody of his children, as their mother had a history of abandoning them and then reclaiming them for short periods. "The county court judge, however, made it clear during the early part of the case that he believed a child's place was with his mother and, no surprise, ruled in her favour. My client felt with good reason that he hadn't had a proper hearing. This is an example of a judge who had made up his mind and wasn't prepared to listen to anything else."

Books from Vision

An extract from
Power and Corruption
by Stephen Moore

...It is the sort of situation which would warrant the immediate despatch of James Bond 007 – an idyllic island in the Caribbean is taken over by a sinister criminal organisation.

In one of Ian Fleming's novels it would have been the evil organisation SPECTRE which seizes control. Bond would have despatched the villains with the help of a Walther PPK, a gorgeous girl on his arm and a vodka martini at the bar.

Yet the reality in the 1990s is just as dramatic.

The beautiful Caribbean island of Aruba, only five miles wide and 20 miles long, was 'bought' by elements of the Sicilian Mafia along with its 65,000 inhabitants. Everything of importance on the island was taken over by the mobsters, controlling elements of the police, politicians, customs and, most importantly, the banks. The 'ownership' of their own State offered wonderful opportunities for corruption on a previously unthinkable scale. Its very existence was founded on corruption and criminality.

Aruba lies just off the Venezuelan coast. During the age of discovery and conquest it was ignored by the Spanish, who described it as 'barren and useless', despite its beautiful long white beaches, and instead it fell into the hands of the Dutch and became part of the six Dutch Antilles.

Sleepy and ignored it was the perfect off-shore Shangri-La for the Mafia. For years they kept their ownership quiet, transforming Aruba into a staging post for cocaine smuggling. At the same time they bribed officials and used the island's banks to launder their money – channelling vast sums obtained from drugs, extortion, murder and prostitution across the world.

The authorities only discovered the Mafia's presence after a dramatic and violent police raid on offices in Caracas, the capital of Venezuela. Investigators seized computer disks concerning deals involving the Cuntreras family, one of the most dangerous Sicilian

Mafia clans. The Cuntreras had been living in Venezuela for years and visiting Aruba for lengthy holidays. But the disks and other documents showed they had been doing more in the Caribbean than soaking up the sun.

The information seized by the police proved that more than 60% of businesses and economic life on Aruba was owned and controlled by the Mafia.

When the American authorities belatedly realised what was going on there was little they could do. One of their most expensive satellites was moved off course to 'sit' on top of the island and spot smugglers boats and cocaine drops in the ocean, but it was a difficult task even when the clouds allowed vision. One of the largest hauls of cocaine ever discovered in Britain came via Aruba.

Investigators came to the conclusion that the Mafia wanted Aruba not only to create the perfect base for corruption and crime, but also as a bolt-hole they could flee to when they needed to escape the law and avoid extradition to America, Europe or, more specifically, Italy.

Their fears soon seemed justified. In September 1992 Venezuela agreed to extradite back to Italy three of the most dangerous Cuntreras brothers: Guiseppe, Pasquale and Paulo, a trio known as the Black Emperors and reputedly worth more than $1 billion each, earned from drugs. Back home they were arrested and thrown into Italy's top-security Pianosa prison.

Investigators claim the Black Emperors took part in the appalling murder of Judge Giovanni Falcone, who was blown up shortly after he arranged for their extradition to Italy. They then assassinated Paulo Borsellino, Falcone's successor.

According to the US Drug Enforcement Agency the Cuntreras were the main force behind the acquisition of Aruba, a buying spree which started in the early 1980s, when the Black Emperors were frequent visitors to the island with their 'beautiful' wives. They stayed at first in Spartan accommodation, were kind to their kids and avoided ostentatious displays of wealth, according to locals. Meanwhile they were arranging the purchase of restaurants, banks, hotels, cafés, and every type of local business.

Organised crime was hardly a newcomer to the region. From the arrival of pirates and buccaneers centuries ago to the more recent arrivals of fugitive financiers and money launderers, every criminal wants a home in the Caribbean. The island was quick to welcome the latest arrivals with their new investment and the Aruba government took little action, perhaps through fear of reprisals. Exceptionally, one member of the gang was arrested in 1988 and the Aruban authorities requested military assistance from Holland as protection. The Dutch took the request seriously and sent a frigate and a force of soldiers.

The Aruba experience shows that while the Mafia's global power has been under attack, the income from organised crime, the ability to hide it, to launder it and the ability to use it for corruption still poses great threats to international order...

Books from Vision

Books from Vision

An extract from Price of Power by Colin Challen

...As soon as the election was over, Major threw himself on his sword as expected. The ensuing leadership contest was remarkable not only for its bitterness, which further crystalised the Conservative Party's divisions over Europe – but also for the amount of money spent on the candidates' campaigns. With an actual electorate of only 164 MPs, the candidates managed to spend around £250,000 between them – roughly £150 per head. The eventual winner, William Hague, at £110,100, managed to spend more than twice as much as any one of his rivals. The bulk of Hague's finance came from Harris Ventures Ltd – Lord Harris of Peckham, the carpet millionaire's company. He gave £74,000, and was to be rewarded with the Treasurership of the party. Harris, whose company Harris Queensway went bust in 1988, had climbed back up the ladder of corporate donors. In 1992, he paid the salaries of two Central Office staff, although reports suggested he was rather coy about his support becoming public knowledge.[1]

The next most generous Hague supporter, coming in at £20,000, was David Steene, who was managing director of City Mortgage Corporation (CMC). In July of 1997 CMC came under fire for its excessive interest charges and redemption penalties. These meant for example that if a borrower missed one payment, the interest rates could double. CMC targetted the poor, the self employed and council house purchasers. One couple, who were evicted from their home, found that their £150 monthly payment for a £15,000 loan went up to £500 after one instalment was missed. Eventually, a CMC Victim's Association was established, and over 1,000 customers were considering taking legal action for redress. Steene said, "I am always concerned to hear of customers that have any problems with their loan."[2] The Office of Fair Trading, however, was moved to issue guidance prohibiting dual rates of interest and practices which were 'deceitful, oppressive and unfair.'[3] There was nothing unfair or oppressive about Steene's own pay, since in 1996 he was paid by CMC's US parent company, the Cityscape Financial Corporation,

£578,000 for his efforts.[4] Hague presumably felt that none of the controversy surrounding his benefactor's business should rub off on him, since he said it was a 'personal' donation.

The second highest funded leadership campaign was that of John Redwood, who declared expenditure of £55,534.36. £44,000 of this came from the Conservative 2000 campaign, through its trading company, Wilfred Street Conferences and Publications Ltd. The remainder was paid for by the defeated Tory MP for Welwyn, Hatfield, David Evans, a former PPS to Redwood. Michael Howard spent £49,000 almost half of which, £23,500 came from Alan Hagdrup, a former director of Hanson plc. Ken Clarke, deemed by many to have the most gravitas of all the contenders spent a modest £42,000. Bringing up the rear was Peter Lilley, who spent £27,850. Both the Chairman and Treasurer of the Carlton Club's Political Committee, Sir Brian Goswell and Richard Simmons CBE respectively, supported Lilley's campaign.[5]

Hague's appeal – apart from his youth – was that he would bring radical changes to the way the party worked: "I think it is time to choose a leader from the new generation who has conviction and energy to make the changes that are required if we are to win the next general election and become the party of government again" he said.[6] In one respect he was appealing over the heads of the Parliamentary Party to the membership. Most polls had shown in the early stages of the contest that he was ahead of his rivals in constituency support, although this was not borne out in the party's official consultation when constituency chairmen plumped decisively for Ken Clarke.

Hague's election as leader in June was quickly followed by headlines which proclaimed he was to 'get tough' on sleaze. He made a speech on the 23rd July proclaiming 'The Six Principles of Renewal' which were Unity, Decentralisation, Democracy, Involvement, Integrity and Openness. The last – and least – of these dealt with the party's funding. Hague said:

". . we must be open about our funding. In not being so in the past, we have often appeared secretive and defensive. And we have paid a political price for that. It is time to be much more open. We have nothing to hide and nothing to fear."

"And so I will instruct our Party treasurers that in future years we will list the major donors to the Conservative Party alongside our published accounts. But I want to go further than that. We have to recognise public concern across the Western world about the sources of funding for political parties. We must respond to that concern. We will publish new guidance later this year, and our intention is that in future years the Conservative Party will no longer accept foreign donations."[7]

The first commitment, wrapped-up in the common ploy of alluding to the 'appearance of secretiveness' – as opposed to the party's actual strict policy of secretiveness – suggests perhaps that the public got it wrong about the party 'with nothing to hide or fear.' The principle of secrecy, which had been protected religiously for the whole life of the party had after all been something which John Major had defended ad nauseum at the Dispatch Box until the very end. The right of an individual to financially support the party of his or her choice in complete privacy was enshrined as if it were a basic civil liberty on a par with the secret ballot.

It was not long after his election to the leadership, according to the press, that Hague had to go cap in hand to 'Tyke tycoons' in his native county, to get £2 million to tide the party over until the annual conference in September. It was reported that although the party had come out of the election campaign with a small surplus, it was unable to raise sufficient funds to cover its estimated £500,000 per month running costs.[8] In August, Hague appointed two new treasurers, Sir Graham Kirkham as senior treasurer, with Michael Ashcroft as his deputy. Between them, it was estimated the two men had a combined fortune of nearly £500 million.[9] For Ashcroft, his appointment realised a long held ambition – he had, it seemed, coveted a party treasurer's post at least since 1991, after Alastair McAlpine gave up the job, but he was unfortunately getting a bad press at the time due to accusations about his business practices, which he denied. Nevertheless, a Central Office spokesperson was moved to say in regards to a very generous back to back loan from Ashcroft: "I have to add that if Mr Ashcroft has in any way broken any laws of the country, then the money goes back to him straight away. This party is clean."[10] This rather wide-ranging commitment was later refined to the narrower standard response, following the Nadir debacle, that only stolen money would be returned. Ashcroft's problem was not that he was in anyway breaking any laws – he wasn't – but that the City found him 'too clever by half.'[11] The complexity of his business dealings, coupled with his activities in the former British colony of Belize gave the impression of a secretive political schemer. When he sold his company ADT on the day of the general election, he reportedly made £154 million.

One of Hague's alleged Yorkshire millionaire targets was Paul Sykes, who had earlier demonstrated his generosity to the party by sponsoring the election expenses of scores of Euro-sceptical candidates, and who had chosen Lord Parkinson to sit on the board of his computer company, Planet Online. Sykes' support of the Euro-sceptics led to criticisms of 'cash for policies' since he had set up a £500,000 "fighting fund for candidates prepared to pledge in their manifestos that they are against the single currency."[12] Sykes said that by early April, 1967 candidates had been in touch with him, and since 147 of them had already made up their minds about the single currency, his offer could hardly be described as a 'bribe.' In addition, he was reported to have given the party centrally a 'significant' donation to general funds. He said "My country's worth everything I have got. I never start out on something I cannot finish. And I am not going to run out of money."[13] By the day of the election, Sykes was said to have given between £1,000 and £3,000 to 237 Tory candidates. On the eve of the election the Guardian reported that in some cases the size of the donation under new parliamentary rules would mean that if the candidate was elected as the MP, he or she may not be allowed to speak on behalf of the cause for which the money was expressly donated. Thus it was that by polling day, the headline ran "Tories may repay Sykes" – but by then, the damage had been done. At the same time, in his own name, Sykes was running full-page advertisements in the press, urging Britain to "WAKE UP TO THE FACTS" and vote Conservative. He must have assumed that the previous press coverage had acquainted the electorate with who he was, since in one advertisement, simply entitled "A personal message from Paul Sykes," there was no explanation as to his background.[14]

The Sykes money had overtones of an earlier Euro-sceptical donation row, which had enveloped the doyen of the Conservative backbench sceptics, Bill Cash. His 'European Foundation' received money from the late Sir James Goldsmith back in 1996, coincidentally at the same time as Cash was introducing a Euro Referendum Bill in the Commons. Cash denied that there was any connection, but it was embarrassing for John Major to have linked in the public's mind

78 of his backbenchers who supported Cash's bill appearing to ally themselves with the Goldsmith line, incidentally leading to speculation that they were as much concerned with protecting their seats from Sir James' Referendum Party as voting for any matter of principle. But those 78 had also set the seal on the future Euro-sceptical course of the party, leading to Hague's succession to the leadership.

Books from Vision

INDEX

Index

Index

Index

Index